Does Anything Matter? Why a Christian should still care in a world of despair

Ronald JJ Wong

Published by Ronald JJ Wong, 2024.

Table of Contents

.... 1
Synopsis 3
Endorsements 4
What matters? 11
Pro Bono 12
What's Matter? 18
Humanity's Existential Crisis 22
Does Everything In Between Matter? 26
Do You Matter? 34
Does Your Work Matter? 44
Work that illumines 45
To Work and Keep all that God has made 51
Keeping the Word Matters 61
The Work We Create Matters 66
Does Loving Your Neighbour Matter? 69
Who is your neighbour? 70
Will you be a neighbour? Between compassion and diversion 72
How Can You Be a Neighbour? 79
Mercy Matters 85
What If You Care Too Much? A Paralysis of Despair 90
What Matters to Keep Us Going? 102
What Will All We Do Amount To? Fruitfulness & Faithfulness 112
What Impact? 113
Faithfulness brings Fruitfulness 116
God is the vine dresser 118
Jesus is the true vine 120
The command to obey 123
God's orchestration towards fruitfulness 124
God-Orchestrated 128
What fruitfulness is 130

Faithfulness of a few to the fruitfulness of many 131
Faithful in the dark 133
Your joy will be full 138
Prayer For Those Who Choose to Continue the Struggle with Doubt, Despair or Futility 141
Support 143

Does Anything Matter?
Why a Christian should still care in a world of despair

Ronald JJ Wong

Does Anything Matter? Why a Christian should still care in a world of despair

Copyright © Ronald JJ Wong, 2024
Published by Ronald JJ Wong
www.ronaldjjwong.com
All rights reserved.

No part of this publication may be reproduced, stored in a retrieval system or transmitted, in any form or by any means, electronic, mechanical, photocopying, recording or otherwise, without the prior permission of the copyright owner.

Scripture quotations are from the ESV® Bible (The Holy Bible, English Standard Version®), © 2001 by Crossway, a publishing ministry of Good News Publishers. Used by permission. All rights reserved. The ESV text may not be quoted in any publication made available to the public by a Creative Commons license. The ESV may not be translated in whole or in part into any other language.

Scripture quotations marked (NLT) are taken from the Holy Bible, New Living Translation, copyright ©1996, 2004, 2015 by Tyndale House Foundation. Used by permission of Tyndale House Publishers, Carol Stream, Illinois 60188. All rights reserved.

Synopsis

Are you grappling with self-doubt or feeling disheartened about your work or ministry? Do you question the purpose of your daily tasks or the impact of your acts of service, compassion, or justice-seeking? Do you ever wonder if your efforts to care for, serve, visit, pray with, or assist others truly make a difference?

You're not alone. As a father, husband, bi-vocational church elder leader, mentor, lawyer, workplace leader, preacher, writer, missions mobilizer, social service practitioner, advocate, and friend, I too wrestle with the heavy burden of perceived failure in fulfilling these roles.

So, what keeps us going? How can we persevere in faith, discipleship, vocation, and ministry? Why should we persist in embodying justice and mercy in a culture riddled with division, conflict, existential despair, climate anxiety, and even talk of species suicide? What can we cling to when hopelessness threatens to overwhelm us?

In this book, I intertwine insights from Scripture, theology, philosophy, theoretical physics, and personal experience into a comprehensive reflection. My hope is that this work will serve as a comforting companion to fellow pilgrims navigating similar struggles.

Endorsements

This book contains the honest reflections of a true optimist – someone who has put skin in the game, tasted of the misery of this world, and in spite of (or rather, through) it has found a hope that really matters. This book is a word in season for our generation. It speaks to the intellectual and to the activist; to the world-weary and to the humble child seeking to live faithfully.
Read with care.
Rev Ng Zhi-Wen
Board Chair, Habibi Singapore
Pastor at Zion Bishan Bible-Presbyterian Church, Singapore

RONALD WONG'S BOOK delves into existential questions with poetic clarity, intertwining God, spirituality, and the daily Christian life seamlessly. From cosmic mysteries to everyday moments in a café, he weaves a narrative that draws readers deeper into understanding faith in a world filled with challenges. Each chapter and paragraph is a journey that enriches the soul and fosters a closer walk with God. Dive in and savour the goodness of his insights!
Dr Goh Wei-Leong
Co-Founder, HealthServe
Global Board, OM International & Chairman, Mercy Teams International

International Christian Medical Dental Association
Christian Medical Dental Fellowship (Singapore)

THROUGH THIS BOOK, Ronald extends a gentle invitation to weary travellers to pause, and ponder life's meanderings, with all its associated questions of struggle and purpose. His wise words open a window for us to catch a clearer glimpse of God's goodness and presence within the world, with honest musings drawn from his own experience that breathed fresh insight while tending to old questions. In reading and reflecting, I found myself challenged and encouraged, and moved to continue this journey with hope, whilst also craving a plate of hokkien mee.

Prarthini Selveindran
Fellowship of Evangelical Students Singapore

POST TENEBRAS LUX (After Darkness, Light). That was the motto of some ancient Christians as they rediscovered God in a seemingly hopeless world. Ronald Wong makes the same journey, through his own life, faith, study, and experience. I recommend you read this book devotionally, allowing it to direct you to a place of honest prayer with your Maker. And perhaps afterward, to a grilled cheese sandwich.

Rev Dr Dev Menon
Pastor, Zion Bishan BP Church
Author of The Rest Race and The Pattern: Discovering God's Design for Marriage

THE QUESTION "DOES anything matter?" is deeply relevant for this present age where our understanding of personal value and vocation is so unmoored and untethered. In this book, Ronald JJ Wong vulnerably reflects on his varied experiences across different arenas of life, ushering the reader through a tender, meditative journey to answer that question. Winsomely thoughtful, biblically mature, and gracefully poetic — this book will shine a gentle, guiding light onto the reader's path. It is my pleasure to commend it with enthusiasm.

Ps Leow Wen Pin
Chairman, Koinonia Inclusion Network, Singapore

IF YOU'VE EVER FELT discouraged by all that's going on in the world and wondered why what you do matters, this book is for you. Through biblical scripture, practical applications and vulnerable, riveting stories, Ronald will take you on a journey that infuses you with hope to live with purpose for Christ, in a world filled with despair. A beautiful, poignant read.

Dr Tam Wai Jia
Founder, Kitedreams Global

MANY CHRISTIANS LIVE in two worlds: one sacred - during the weekends, and the other secular during Mondays to Fridays. God being the Lord in the former, but conspicuously absent in the latter. What Ronald Wong's book demonstrates, however, is that God is the Lord of every nook and corner of His Creation, not just over our churches and weekends. He does so elegantly by weaving together reflections on a myriad of his passions and interests: from nature, social justice, quantum physics and poetry to cheese sandwiches, Christian discipleship, mental health and how to be good neighbours. The net result is a poetic tapestry that reminds all Christians to seek to live integrative lives faithful to God.

Dr Lai Pak Wah
Principal and Lecturer,
Church History and Marketplace Theology
Biblical Graduate School of Theology

IN THIS BOOK, THE AUTHOR who is a lawyer, a philosopher, a poet, a preacher, an activist, a science geek, a nature lover, a father, a husband, a preacher, and an octopus(?!) grapples with perplexing questions of life. Ronald Wong has always been regarded as an astute intellectual, able to grasp and articulate difficult theoretical concepts. In this book, he reveals that he is also a contemplative feeler. I love his personal anecdotes and can identify with several of them. This book made me chuckle, led me to ponder in awe, and moved me to tears. Most importantly, this book made me feel I am not alone with all my questions, doubts and despair as a believer and minister of Christ. I will read it again.

Rick Toh
Lead Pastor, Yio Chu Kang Chapel

DOES THIS BOOK MATTER?

Those of us who traverse life with heavier steps will likely find Ronald's wanderings a familiar landscape.

Equipped with the lamp of God's word, strapped up with tight theology, leaning on the staff of philosophy, taking bearings from theoretical physics, (and not forgetting a backpack filled with personal vignettes which include stringy cheese toast), Ronald guides us through the thickets of doubt, over the bogs of despair, across the cliff of hopelessness, and finally, onto the precipice of clarity. Fittingly, here, we get on our knees and praise our almighty triune God when we behold the glory of His hand. Like life, the journey through the pages is not simple. But it will be fruitful, by the grace of Christ.

If you are a sojourner, you need to read this. If you resonate more as a seeker, then perhaps, you need to read this even more.
Wilson Chan
Managing Director, Skillseed

OUR EFFORTS – TO DO good, raise the next generation well, improve the world – can feel so futile with uncertain outcomes. Ronald helps us all to grapple with this reality with clear-eyed insights from Scripture, powerful personal stories and revelations from science. This book will deepen you, if you let it, shifting you to a new space of faith, hope and love.
Jenni Ho-Huan
Pastor, Author, Founder of To Really Live

AT THE CLIMACTIC END of "Bohemian Rhapsody" by Freddie Mercury, hardly audible are the words, "Nothing really matters to me". Ronald Wong asks the question, "Does anything matters?" and brings together philosophy, science, theology—and personal experience—to make a case for a world "not of God playing dice, but of God conducting an orchestra at cosmic scale to His symphony". For all the reasons to doubt and despair, this book offers us hope that we and what we do matter, just as every part of the orchestra contributes to the divine symphony."

Rev Dr David Wong
General Secretary, Bible-Presbyterian Church in Singapore

THERE IS MUCH IN THE news and on social media today that can lead a person into despair, existential and otherwise. In response to these challenges, Ronald J.J. Wong brings us through Scripture, theology, philosophy, theoretical physics and his own personal experience to help us make sense of the world we live in. As he does this, he challenges us to respond in faithful discipleship, remembering who we are in Christ and living the "post-resurrection New Creation life." And he shares relatable ways of being faithful that lead to fruitfulness. Indeed, he helpfully suggests that "when a Christian does a small act of love unto the Lord, ... it is a foretaste of New Creation for the person who experiences that love." I commend this book to thoughtful readers who want to believe that everything we do truly matters to God.

Rev Ivan Tan
Pastor, Fairfield Methodist Church

RONALD WONG IS BOTH an observer of life and an activist. This book is an intersection of both these aspects of who he is, as he asks the big questions of life - do I matter? and if I do, how do I keep going on? Weaving together scripture, theology, science, and metaphysics in no particular pattern, as well as his photographs and prayers, he suggests and inspires answers so that we can live meaningfully every day.

Dr Kwa Kiem Kiok

Lecturer in the areas of mission and intercultural studies at Singapore Bible College

I'VE KNOWN RONALD FOR years and it's no surprise to me that I share the sentiment of all he has written in this book. And yet, his personal stories, words and contemplations in this book have to be one of the most honest I've ever heard from him.

By his honesty, I am reminded of our common human experience; the ordinary human pain of existence which often leaves us with the confronting question: 'Why bother (with what we do)?' But this a difficult question to recognise in our lives, let alone admit to asking (deep inside) - perhaps especially for those who have already made firm commitments in various arenas of their lives, and who may believe that simply asking that question demonstrates a lack of faith.

As Ronald reminds us through this book, it is not.

The articulation of our struggle, our tension, and the pain of what is unspoken in our hearts is healing in its own way. Much like the friend I've found in Ronald, this book is indeed a "comforting companion" to explore and navigate these difficult terrains with, so that we can continue to find hope, and strength for the days ahead, and to remain faithful to the end.

Jonathan Cho
Lawyer, Elder (Bethesda Frankel Estate Church)

What matters?

Pro Bono

His ashen eyes stared straight through the screen.

John[1] was in prison, held in remand. I was speaking to him on a video call to understand his case and to offer him pro bono legal representation. I had been asked to help him on short notice. His court hearing was the next day. And he was going to plead guilty and be sentenced then.

John recounted to me what transpired during the altercation at the homeless shelter he was at. Without guile, like a seasoned veteran, he firmly admitted to the acts alleged in the criminal charges.

Unfortunately, he had lost his job. His wife and two young children lived in Indonesia. His daughter had been having asthmatic symptoms. They've been going from doctor to doctor to figure out what's wrong and paying hefty medical fees every month. Since he was arrested, he had hoped he could be out on bail to work, earn some income and continue to provide for his family. But he didn't have the means to post bail. He had no one who could do so for him.

After I ran through the legal matters, mitigation points and possible sentence, he said to me, "can you do me a favour? Can you contact my wife and tell her I'm okay—once I'm out I'll look for her and we will plan our life forward together. Don't worry so much; leave it to God... My wife has depression since giving birth to our second child."

I told him I'd arrange it.

At the end of our meeting, I offered to pray with him, which he gladly accepted.

After the meeting, my team and I rushed to work on his case. We researched relevant sentencing cases and prepared points for his mitigation plea and legal submissions on sentence. My teammate worked through the night on the submissions and cases.

The next day, at the court mention, the Deputy Public Prosecutor ("DPP") prosecuting his charges argued for 10-13 weeks' imprisonment for his offences. Based on some possibly relevant sentencing cases, we argued for 4 weeks. As he has been in remand since his arrest 1 month ago, we were hoping that a short prison sentence meant that after backdating the sentence to when he was first in remand, he would be released that very day to reunite with his family.

The DPP played a video from the police officer's body camera. It was apparent that John was intoxicated with alcohol and was aggressively shouting and cursing at the police officers, pushing the hands of one of them away. It was jarring to watch. I felt a knot of disappointment swell up in my bowels.

The judge, after hearing all the submissions, decided on 9 weeks' imprisonment in total, backdated to when John was first in remand.

It felt like in the final analysis, it came down to a number. An arithmetic operation calculated with reference to two ends of a numerical spectrum.

What was the point of my team's involvement? It hardly made a difference. The outcome could possibly have been the same if we didn't represent John. At most, 1 week's difference. When it was a matter of 9 or 10 weeks, 1 week seemed insignificant.

Did it matter? Did our pro bono legal representation matter? 'Pro bono' literally means 'public good'. Did we do any good to John? Did we do any good to the public? Did we matter?

Did I matter?

THERE WAS A SEASON where my wife and I opened our home to house a former sex worker.

The request came from Sarah*, the leader of a ministry and a friend. The ministry reaches out to sex workers in Geylang and journeys with them through a long road of transformation, including caring for the family, life and vocational reskilling, counselling, and discipleship. The word got out to some of us that a lady they were journeying with needed to be hosted in a home for a while because there had been a flare up with her abusive partner. My wife and I discussed and decided to offer our home, since we had a spare room at the time.

The first evening, we welcomed the lady to our home and provided a simple dinner for her. I'll refer to her as "Kay"*. We chatted and showed Kay around the flat. She was visibly shy and nervous around us, being a stranger in someone else's home. However, she conveyed to Sarah that she liked our place and liked us (enough, I suppose).

The next four months turned out to be a roller coaster.

Kay would often stay out till very late and not update anyone about her whereabouts, causing all of us to worry. One day, she did not come back. Sarah eventually managed to contact her and found out that Kay had decided to return to her abusive partner. Her belongings were still at our place, so Sarah requested that we leave them there temporarily. The next thing we knew, Kay was pregnant with her partner's child. Not long after, however, we were told that her partner had another violent episode. She needed a home again.

We welcomed her back to our place. Yet, because of my wife's and my lifestyles and other commitments at the time, we could not be home every day to be a constant presence for Kay. We did make clear to Sarah our constraints, but she and Kay understood and agreed.

Four months after she first showed up at our door, Kay again did not come home for several days. Again, Sarah tried unsuccessfully at first to contact her. Eventually, after she managed to reach Kay, she found out that Kay had decided to go back to her partner.

During that season, I experienced several rounds of cycles of emotions from disappointment to frustration to guilt to doubt to resignation. At some point, I wondered if, to shield myself from appreciating fully the futility of all that we–that is, the whole circle of care in Kay's life–were doing, I had simply numbed myself and chosen to believe that nothing we did mattered.

Did anything we do ever matter?

What's Matter?

"Matter" has multiple faces.

Matter is that which is important, when "matter" is understood as a stative verb, that is, a verb which describes a state of being. If you say to me that I matter, does it then describe my *being* or my *doing*?

Or matter may be understood as a *potentiality* which, according to Aristotle, given the right form, becomes *substance*. Maybe I do matter, only because I am presently without substance. Just a transient state in search of something which holds me together.

Or matter as the fundamental building block of the universe. Having mass and volume. I suppose I matter if I take up space in this universe. And have inertia. I do have lots of it, being resistant to change or movement. After all, mass is, in classical physics, related to force and change in momentum.

I think of Isaac Newton, who gave the world the fundamental laws of classical mechanics. The famous three laws of motion. The second of which is that force is mass multiplied by acceleration.

Legend has it that this insight arose after an apple fell on his head. This apple incident supposedly happened when he was forced to go home on a two-year hiatus after a bubonic plague broke out in the University of Cambridge, where he was a student at. Prior to that, he was not a stellar student. An underachiever, apparently.[2]

Somehow, meditating under an apple tree while forced to take a two-year vacation changed the course of his life. And ours too. In the end, he mattered.

HOWEVER, IF NEWTON'S laws of motion were all that mattered, we would be, as a human species, a very different thing. Because most of humanity would probably believe in hard or causal determinism. Everything has been pre-determined by cause and effect. If the universe is nothing but physical matter, and physical matter obeys nothing but the laws of classical mechanics, everything follows the physical laws of cause and effect.

A rock would have rolled down Mount Everest because something caused it to, which itself was caused by something else. The whole chain of causation would be traced back to the Big Bang. Nothing would be outside of this chain of cause and effect. Including the neurons in my brain transmitting impulses that give rise to thoughts, emotions and intentions, which then make me cough out words I think I am creating and make my hands write the words. But in fact, it would be the necessary physical consequence of a myriad of past physical events.[3]

Apart from the issue of holding people accountable for their actions, there is also the issue of agency. Do people really have the moral choice to do anything? Is there a point in us doing anything at all?[4]

Someone like John would have been predetermined by the unintentional physical forces of the universe to make certain choices which would land him where he ended up, right? Homeless. Jobless. Intoxicated. In an altercation. In jail.

Nothing I did would have changed that. Nothing done by the charity who runs the homeless shelter would have changed that. It would all have been futile. Right?

Humanity's Existential Crisis

I recall having a conversation with Derek* over lunch about not having children.

Derek is several years younger than me. A professional acquaintance introduced by my colleague. We were having chicken stew in a cafe by a window which looked out onto the Singapore river. We talked about his memorable work experience and professional aspirations. At some point, we talked about our personal life. He mentioned that he is married without children.

I asked him if he and his wife were planning on having children. He looked up at me, smiled faintly, and said, "We thought about it and decided we will not have children. This world is so messed up. It is so unequal, racist, sexist, and prejudiced. We don't want to bring another person into it and add to the problem."

Up until that time, I had not heard anyone tell me something like that. I had however read about this rising trend among younger people. Much of it is apparently attributable to climate anxiety, a despair at the future of earth in the light of the climate crisis. In 2021, a research study found that 40% of young people from 10 different countries were hesitant to have children because of the climate crisis. Over 45% felt that their negative feelings about climate change affected their daily life and functioning.[5]

In Singapore, many young people do not want to have children because of concerns about cost of living, climate change and other global issues, and their careers and lifestyles being impacted.[6]

It is as if human beings are set on collective suicide as a species. The idea of species suicide is not new. The same kind of anxiety and self-destructive impulse plagued people during the Cold War era when the spectre of nuclear annihilation hung over everyone. The environmental movement which grew in momentum from the 1960s, coupled with the introduction of contraceptive pills, led many people, especially young women, to declare unto themselves they would not have children in such a dirty world. Prior to, the Holocaust and the two Great Wars made many despair of life. I imagine that the era of the Industrial Revolution would have been no better.

It seems then that at many points in human history, people have had great reasons to despair and harbour the desire to commit species suicide. Perhaps an analogy with individual suicide gives us another perspective on this. People commit suicide to end a state of anxiety; to go; not to change things; to want the hurting to stop—this was the conclusion of an anthropologist Charles McDonald. In another study investigating the Kulbi people in Palawan, Philippines, he found that the young were exposed to many suicide occurrences and had come to see it as acceptable behaviour. McDonald thus came up with a "wave hypothesis"—any turbulence would cause a wave of suicides.[7]

Suicide contagion is known as the Werther effect, named after the protagonist in Goethe's 18th century novel The Sorrows of Young Werther. In the story, Werther ended his life after falling in love with a married woman. After it was published, hundreds of copy-cat suicides happened across Germany. Such human suggestibility to suicide transcends time and cultures. In South Korea, studies found that public suicides soared by about 16% just the day after the media reports a celebrity's suicide. Researchers and experts have thus called for media regulation regarding suicide reporting.[8]

Perhaps an analogy could be drawn here. After all, the media would hardly find it newsworthy to report that certain couples have decided to try and conceive because these couples believe, against the backdrop of climate anxiety and despair, that there is yet hope. And having and raising a child in this broken world is a testament to that hope. Likewise, those who choose to foster or adopt and raise a child. It is similarly a courageous act of hope. A painstaking labour of sowing into the future.

It is to bring about the potentiality for change. With the right form, that is, climate consciousness and values formation, there will be substance for this hope. Hopefully, prayerfully, a child who would grow up to be a giver and not only a consumer.

Yet, for many people, they would choose otherwise. Given a choice, they would probably choose not to have lived at all. They would choose to have neither any beginning nor end. Does nothing really matter at all, that there is no worth in beginning or continuing anything to their end?

Does Everything In Between Matter?

If you knew that you'd go through all the disappointment, sleepless nights, frustration, heartache, and sorrow, would you have chosen to do it in the beginning?

Some days, I think of what would happen if my spouse were stricken with, say, severe dementia, stroke and terminal cancer all at once. And then after a long ordeal, she passes. And I am left alone to face the ruins of our life.

Or I imagine my presently 3-year-old child being struck with multiple sclerosis and muscular dystrophy, diminishing every day before my very eyes, with his limbs and organs wasting away until there will eventually be nothing left but dry bones.

Or I think of the times he is having a tempestuous meltdown in the middle of the road. Or when he is wailing and vomiting on his bed every half hour throughout the night.

Would I have chosen to begin at all? Knowing that somewhere between the beginning and the end, there is waiting and agonising and there is suffering.

Would I choose, if I had the choice, such a life again? Would I have chosen to marry? Would I have chosen to have my child?

How could I not? How could I ever choose to have never known them?

I think of God who made everything in the beginning.

He knew at the beginning how the world He would make would all shatter. Broken fragments would make a thousand cuts to His heart. But He still did it. He still chose to make the world.

Knowing full well the pain it would bring Him, God chose to make a beginning for the universe, for us, for you. For your life story.

He is the God of beginnings.

"In the beginning, God / was the Word": Genesis 1:1; John 1:1.

God was there at the beginning. God is there at the end of this age. God is here in the present.

From our perspective, God *is* with us in time; God was with us at the beginning of our life; God *was* before we were even a fragment of thought in His mind; God *will be* there with us in our tomorrow, long after our last breath on earth.

From another perspective, God is *outside time*. God is the one who made the twirling cycles of time, the luminescent spectrum of night and day, the summers that scorch and winters that howl, the sticky showers and the cool rain of our tropics.

Frederick Buechner wrote in a sermon "Air for Two Voices":[9]

> ""In the beginning," he says, "was the Word," and although it is a poem he is writing, we assume that he is being more than just poetic. "In principio," he says, and we assume he means no less than what Genesis means with *bereshith*, which is to say "in the beginning" quite literally: before anything yet had been made that was to be made, before whatever it was that happened to make it possible for Being to happen. You can't speak literally about such things, of course, but we assume that he is speaking as seriously as physicists also speak seriously about the possibility at least of a time beyond time before creation happened. At that point where everything was nothing or nothing everything, before the Big Bang banged or the Steady State was stated, when there was no up and no down, no life and no death, no here and no there, at the very beginning, John says, there was this

Word, which was God and through which all things were made.

The Bible is usually very universal and makes you want to see something—some image to imagine it by. "The light shines in the darkness," John says, and maybe you see an agonizing burst of light with the darkness folding back like petals, like hands. But the imagery of John is based rather on sound than on sight. It is a Word you hear breaking through the unimaginable silence—a creating word, a word that calls forth, a word that stirs life and is life because it is God's word, John says, and has God in it as your words have you in them, have in them your breath and spirit and tell of who you are. Light and dark, the visual, occur in space, but sound, this Word spoken, occurs in time and starts time going. "Let there be," the Word comes, and then there is, creation is. Something is where before there was nothing, and the morning stars sing together and all the Sons of God shout for joy because sequence has begun, time has begun, a story has begun."

Modern science tells us that time is not in fact an independent physical measure of reality. When we remove our human perception from the equation, there is no such thing as objective time. There is spacetime, a mathematical model of the fourth dimension. But other than that, time is almost irrelevant. The arrow of time is merely something we humans *feel*. And the only thing that distinguishes the past and the future is heat or entropy. Entropy is the measure of disorder in a system. Heat is the effect of disorder in subatomic particles. Disorder is chaos.

Everything degenerates towards chaos and disorder without something maintaining order. The past is different from the future in that what has been subject to chaos cannot be reversed on its own. A swinging ball will keep swinging forever to and fro if not for heat or chaos; and you would not be able to distinguish its past and future. But heat or chaos causes it to slow down. Or chaos causes it to be deflated. Then on its own, the ball cannot continue to swing indefinitely. Its future is the death of its movement.

God sits *outside* all of this. God calms the chaos and brings order to disorder by speaking His word to separate one thing from another.

God spoke and separated light from darkness.

Separated the heavens from the earth.

Separated land from the seas.

Separated different types of trees, and plants, and fruits, and seeds.

Separated the sun, and the moon, and the stars.

Separated the different types of flying creatures, and the sea creatures, and the land creatures.

God spoke and created people and separated them: male and female.

By God's word, disorder was dispelled, and order emerged. Like a sapling breaking through the dirt.

God spoke and started the cosmic clock.

God the Son, Jesus, sustains all things. Holds all things together.

"And he (Jesus) is before all things, and in him all things hold together": Colossians 1:17.

"He (Jesus) is the radiance of the glory of God and the exact imprint of his nature, and he upholds the universe by the word of his power": Hebrews 1:3.

The God of beginnings is the God of making things right; the God holding all things together. The God of new beginnings.

I THINK OF THE SECOND night after my wife and I returned home from the hospital after she had just given birth to our child. We were in bed trying to get some sleep when she sat up and shook me. "I'm having bad chest tightness, and I can't breathe," she said. Being the medically untrained folks we are, the first thing we did was to Google the symptoms and read, as we would all do, about the worst-case scenarios. Postpartum cardiomyopathy was a possible condition. Essentially, it's heart failure after childbirth.

With that threat looming over us, we immediately sped to the hospital's Accident & Emergency (A&E) department. We left our new-born child at home with the confinement nanny. It was during a time when the world was still battling the Covid-19 pandemic. Strict Covid measures were still in place. After waiting for some time, my wife finally went in to see the doctor. But I could not go in with her. I sat on a lone loose chair outside the building, next to the drive-in road which turned into the compound.

I waited and waited. I saw the tired night turn into a grey morning. I watched the hospital staff stream in on bicycles and on foot for their morning shift. A dense cloud of a myriad possible scenarios swirled in my mind, all of them tragic.

When my wife finally came out, she told me that the doctor wanted to admit her and run multiple tests on her because they did not know what's wrong with her and there could indeed be a risk of heart failure. And she had to go in alone. No visitors. Then, she went back in to speak further with the doctor.

At that moment, I saw my world shatter. Into a thousand broken fragments. I imagined my wife lying singularly in the hospital bed, dying alone. I imagined myself a widower with a wailing new-born child having to bury my wife. I could feel tears about to erupt. But I tried to suck it in. And I kept saying to myself, "Hold it together. Hold it together. Hold it together." I had to hold it together for my wife and family.

I sat down and texted my friend to tell him what's happening. He replied shortly after:

"Prayed for you bro. Sensed this word for you: "He holds you together" - you as a husband and father, [your wife's] bodily constitution, your family unit. He holds you together and is faithful, and strong to do so.

"For by him all things were created, in heaven and on earth, visible and invisible, whether thrones or dominions or rulers or authorities—all things were created through him and for him. And he is before all things, and in him all things hold together." (Col 1:16-17)".

Then I cried.

God alone was in control, holding everything, even me, together.

(Just so you don't leave wondering what happened to my wife, she is very much alive. She did however go on to struggle with postpartum health issues for about 18 months.)

If you are in a season of waiting, or hoping for a new season, or wondering when the current difficult season will end, wait—wait with hope; wait with faith; wait with confidence; wait with assurance.

Wait on this God of the seasons; this God who is with us in time; this God who sits outside of time; this God who was, and is, and is to come; this God who determines the times and places of each of us. This GOD who holds you together.

Wait on the God of beginnings.

Wait on the God of the in-between.

Wait on the God who holds all things together between the beginning and the end.

Even the in-between matters. As a father, there are some difficult days I wish I could fast forward to the end when my child has grown up, matured, and become independent. Yet, on most days, as I spend time with them growing into the little adult they are destined to become, I cherish the in-between. I miss the early days holding the little infant in my arms soothing them to sleep. I cherish holding them through laughter and tears in their in-between season. So too, I believe, God as He holds us in our in-between.

You may be someone in a help, care, or social service profession, or in a nurturing role, and often wishing you could flip the metaphorical book to the last chapter, whatever that would look like. Skip the disentangling of messy relational conflicts and unearthing of buried trauma in the people you work with. Fast forward the accumulation of marginal growth over long stretches of time and witnessing instantly that one giant leap.

But God, who could have done everything in an instant, chose to separate things into an ordered universe over 6 separate days. Before He made the creatures of various kinds, it was just land and sea, plants and trees, heaven and earth, light and dark. It was good, but *not very good*. Before He made the earth sprout vegetation, plants, and trees, it was just earth, sea, heaven, and light and dark. It was good, *but not very good*. Still, He took His time through each day to make what is good. The in-between matters to Him that He took time to work through them. And still, He holds them all together.

So, even with the mundanity and fatigue of ploughing what seems like barren land, press on. Press on knowing that He is there in the in-between, holding you together.

Do You Matter?

Many days, I doubt myself. I doubt what use I am to the world, to God, or even to myself. I doubt the life trajectory I'm on.

I preach ever so often. In my church and in various churches. It takes me considerable time to prepare each sermon. To dwell on the passage. And dig into the exegesis. And cross-check against commentaries. And craft every sentence. And rewrite every other phrase. And hoping prayerfully that, somehow, what I've written in word, when spoken forth over the pulpit, will be used by God to effect spiritual transformation.

I imagine, and I half suspect every preacher shares this sentiment with me, that at the end of my sermon, the whole congregation will be in tears of repentance and worship. That revival will break out there and then. Erupting from praise into missions to the ends of the earth.

But it never happens. It feels, most of the time, like I'm the Merlion placed in front of a sewage pool: words splatter out of my mouth and trickle into an abyss, disappearing beyond the face of the waters.

Days like that, I stumble into bed in the afternoons after Sunday service and stare blankly at the ceiling fan spin. My mind spirals along with it. I wish it would stop, but not an iota of me can tear me away from that condition of self-doubt.

I know what I've said is making it sound like everything is about me. I don't know. I suppose it's not too much to ask that I get to see or know that there is fruit to my labour. That it is not ultimately an exercise in futility.

DOES ANYTHING MATTER? WHY A CHRISTIAN SHOULD STILL CARE IN A WORLD OF DESPAIR

Strangely, though it may not be much comfort, it seems that even Jesus Himself may have struggled with this. There is that famous verse Matthew 11:28 where Jesus declares "Come to me, all who labor and are heavy laden, and I will give you rest."

The context is that earlier, Jesus' cousin John the Baptist sent his disciples to ask Jesus publicly, "are you the Messiah or should we look for another?" His own cousin and ministry forerunner doubted Him.

Then in Matthew 11:20-24, Jesus began to declare woes on the cities where He had preached and performed great miracles in, but the people did not repent and turn to Him.

Even Jesus experienced a sort of fruitlessness of His ministry. There was great reason, then, to doubt. Doubt the way of God. Doubt the plan of God. Doubt the wisdom of God.

What good is God's wise plans if even God the Son could not succeed with a bunch of stiff-necked Jews from a small town of Capernaum?

Here's a thought about wisdom.

John 1:1: "In the beginning was the Word, and the Word was with God, and the Word was God."

The Greek word for Word is Logos.

For the Greek, the Logos is the cosmic wisdom that orders the universe.

For the Jews, the Logos is the divine revelation of God, who otherwise is so holy He cannot be approached by humans.

The Apostle John declares that Jesus is the Word, the Logos.

Jesus was at the beginning with God.

Jesus was the beginning.

Jesus who is God the Son was with God the Father.

Jesus is and was God the Son. And has always been and always will be.

Jesus is both the wisdom and revelation of God.

Jesus is the source of the wisdom spoken of in the poetic passage in Proverbs 8:22-31:

> "The LORD possessed me (wisdom) at the beginning of his work, the first of his acts of old. Ages ago I was set up, at the first, before the beginning of the earth. When there were no depths I was brought forth, when there were no springs abounding with water. Before the mountains had been shaped, before the hills, I was brought forth, before he had made the earth with its fields, or the first of the dust of the world. When he established the heavens, I was there; when he drew a circle on the face of the deep, when he made firm the skies above, when he established the fountains of the deep, when he assigned to the sea its limit, so that the waters might not transgress his command, when he marked out the foundations of the earth, then I was beside him, like a master workman, and I was daily his delight, rejoicing before him always, rejoicing in his inhabited world and delighting in the children of man."

The wisdom of God can be seen in His design of the universe. Surely, Newton marvelled at God's design when he contemplated the physical laws of motion and gravity. He would not have the chance to learn that God's design is even more marvellous than that. As it turns out, Newton is not the last word on the physical laws of the universe. A major discovery in science which superseded Newtonian physics is quantum physics. What little I do know of it blows my mind. And it should yours.

Subsequent physicists like Niels Bohr, Werner Heisenberg and Erwin Schrödinger discovered that the universe at the subatomic level is unlike anything we had previously understood. Bohr famously said, "Those who are not shocked when they first come across quantum theory cannot possibly have understood it". Even Albert Einstein could not accept it because it was so fantastical, that he famously said, "God does not play dice".

Scientists have come to realise that at the quantum realm, particles have properties and behave in ways which are indeterminate. In Newtonian physics, you could calculate exactly things like the position and velocity of an object given the relevant information. However, in quantum physics, everything is *probabilistic*. You could only calculate the probability that a particle is this or that. Heisenberg concluded that it is impossible to know both the position and momentum of a particle at the same moment with accuracy. Until a particle is in fact measured, it could be everywhere and anywhere. This led to the famous Schrödinger's thought experiment about a cat in a box: until you have peeped into the box, the cat could be both dead and alive. On this, Einstein said to Abraham Pais, "Do you really believe the moon is only there when you look at it?"

So, we do not actually know how or whether any particular outcome will come about in any given system. It is as if there is a constant potentiality waiting to materialise with the right form, and when it does, it does, and we don't know why. And it seems to only materialise when we actually interact with it.

There is yet another twist to this plot. In our day-to-day world, we can measure the speed and position of a ball without affecting those properties. In the quantum realm, even the act of measuring the system itself fundamentally changes its properties. To use the analogy of the cat in the box, once we peep into the box, we have somehow altered the state of affairs within the box!

Then, to add another twist, the properties of subatomic particles are both indeterminate and yet also dependent on one another. This is known as quantum entanglement. In an entangled quantum system, the state of one system is correlated to the state of another, even though individually they each appear to be random. Quantum particles, once entangled, will have states which are strongly correlated no matter the distance between them. It is as though their destinies are irrevocably intertwined once they have encountered one another.

DOES ANYTHING MATTER? WHY A CHRISTIAN SHOULD STILL CARE IN A WORLD OF DESPAIR

ALL OF THAT DOES NOT definitively prove that free will exists. And we don't know if future physicists might discover yet another deeper level of physical laws and systems or larger theory at work. But based on the best scientific evidence we have to date, it tells us that *hard determinism is not proven.*[10]

Free will could exist. And determinism may well be false. Futility from determinism is not a given. It may well be then that we are not trapped in a fixed cycle of cause and effect which we have no control over.[11]

The prevailing theory of the physical universe seems to me to point to a mysterious interwoven fabric where human agency and other forces twirl around one another to make a world that is both ordinarily stable and connected, and yet always ready for the extraordinary to break in.

A physical reality that is anticipating an intertwining with the metaphysical. A world where things matter, every action matters, but are not all trapped in a vicious cycle of cause and effect, of karma. Grace can shift and shape and recreate reality.

A world not of God playing dice, but of God conducting an orchestra at cosmic scale to a beautiful symphony.

If you believe as I do, that God is the one who designed the marvellous and mysterious quantum universe in His wisdom, it can only make us worship Him with greater awe. God in His amazing wisdom created a complex world bound by order yet built on the potentiality of disorder. And it is His love that holds it together. His grace holds together what is otherwise chaos and shapes it into beauty.

Our lives are not so different. It is easy to see our world as chaos and our life as random, but God in His wisdom is the God who shapes beauty out of ash and dust and sets the planets in orbit.

Beauty and order cannot be the children of random chaos.

If you ever doubt the wisdom of God, as you probably already have many times, pause for a moment and look carefully at the works He's made. His creation declares His glory, proclaims His craftsmanship, and displays His wisdom (Psalm 19:1-2).

Something I used to do, and should still do more of, was to pause from work in the mid to late afternoon. I'd have been mentally exhausted from work, tired from the intellectual circles I run around in my head wondering if I got anything I've done so far right. I would go downstairs for a walk. With no destination in mind. Just walk and walk. By the Singapore river. I'd breathe slower. Walk slower. And then I'd sit at the stone steps and look inside. I'd spot the dark grey snakeheads glide lazily by. A faint outline of the clouds hanging above reflected in the green water. This whole liturgy does not solve any problem or answer any question, as much as partaking in Holy Communion does not heal one of diabetes. But it does somehow make me experience in my soul a restfulness—not so much physical rest but resting in the assurance that the wisdom of God, the Divine Logos is more than enough.

Somehow, this liturgy of communing with creation captures my soul afresh to the divine Logos. This liturgy, I commend to you.

After all, Jesus is the architect of the whole universe, the Milky Way, the Solar System and the galaxies. He is also the architect of your life.

Jesus is the author of history, the author of the rise and fall of civilisations and empires. He is also the author of your story.

Jesus is the designer of the fractal in branches of baobab trees, and of the symmetrical octahedral scaffolds of shimmering crystals. He is also the designer of every fibre of your body.

Jesus is the craftsman who sculpted the majestic Grand Canyon. He is also the craftsman who shaped your heart.

Jesus is the artist who paints the heavenly canvas with amber washes and magenta streaks, and also paints every stroke of who you are and who you will become.

And all of this, God in His wisdom created and declared it was good. The Hebrew word used in Genesis 1 is "*towb*", which means good, pleasing, beautiful.

God created you, and you are made good, pleasing, and beautiful.

Yes, you are also broken and imperfect. But you are also redeemed into the New Creation. And it will be good, pleasing, and beautiful.

And so when you question your life, your body, your future, your past, your story, your worth—and it is inevitable that you will question these things at some point in your life, especially when you stumble and fall from an otherwise muted plateau, or when people around you seem to close in on you like circling vultures, or when it feels like life is a meaningless Sisyphean nightmare—look to Jesus, the Word of God, the Divine Logos.

Look to His Word and His Works. Go to a park. Consider the serene water lilies He folds. Consider each leaf of the luscious towering Tembusu tree. Take a walk through your neighbourhood. Smell the nutty caramel scent of the pandan leaves. Gaze at the rich violet garland of bougainvillaea.

The Word who created and crafted those things created, and is recreating, you.

That is why you matter.

DOES ANYTHING MATTER? WHY A CHRISTIAN SHOULD STILL CARE IN A WORLD OF DESPAIR

Does Your Work Matter?

Work that illumines

During a National Service In-Camp Training I was in, some mates and I talked about retirement plans. One mate wanted to be a taxi driver in his retirement, driving people around and chatting with them. Another said he would want to have a role where he could take care of people, including his family. I shared that God willing, I would want to do more mission work, especially cross-culturally. I realised that nobody said they would want to retire and simply laze around or go on a perpetual vacation. Everybody wanted to do something useful in their retirement. That is of course assuming we all would be privileged enough to get to choose to stop working to pay for our basic living expenses.

It reminds me of a senior ex-lawyer formerly from a Big Firm. I caught up with him sometime after he had already retired from lawyering. He had voluntarily retired at an age much earlier than he was expected to. It seemed to his peers and colleagues a rather puzzling choice. He shared though that he wanted to harness his time and energy on other important things. He has been helping to manage a charitable work in Laos and recently started a family ministry in Singapore. In fact, he said, he was busier than before!

For many people, work is a necessary evil. It pays the bills. But if they could choose to not work and still live in luxury, they would be happier for it, so it is assumed. Work is thus a meaningless chore. It has no inherent value.

On the other hand, some people are addicted to their work. Their work defines them. The danger then is that when there are issues at work or with their work performance, their identity and worth are at peril. Work then also has no inherent value because its value is only to feed the ego. Work becomes meaningless when it does not increase one's stature.

I think of the first work. The work which God undertook in the beginning.

"2 The earth was without form and void, and darkness was over the face of the deep. And the Spirit of God was hovering over the face of the waters. 3 And God said, "Let there be light," and there was light": Genesis 1:2-3.

"The light shines in the darkness, and the darkness has not overcome it": John 1:5.

The world was shapeless before God worked it. Strings of particles shivering in erratic waveforms. Darkness was over the face of the deep. Beyond the deep was a plunging void.

Then God spoke. God set ablaze the first light. The light which illuminated the universe, which cannot be looked into but by which everything else could be seen. Light which birthed life. Light which penetrates the deepest crevices of the earth.

This was the work of God. God worked and created, and thus brought order to chaos, direction to disarray, instruction to senselessness, distinction to the monolithic, division to totalitarianism.

JUST AS HUMANITY IS made in the image of God, *human work is an image of God's work.*

Filing binders of letters and documents and shelving them by category and date; keeping a business's ledger; preparing a set of financial accounts; directing a phone enquiry to the right staff in the right department; wiping up coffee grounds spilled all over the countertop; developing and presenting a marketing plan; tending to an elderly patient; cooking a plate of *hokkien mee*.

Human work is an image of God's work in the same way that it brings order to chaos, and light to darkness.

Take the *hokkien mee* for example. Before the chef works it, it is a disarray of raw ingredients—pork bones, prawns, *ikan bilis*, squid, clams, eggs, noodles, chives.

The dish was formless and void, and darkness was over the face of the wok. With the right ingredients in the right order at the right temperature, a dish would emerge, like life birthed at creation.

Then the chef begins working the dish. She turns on the gas stove and set the fire, and there was light. The pork bones, prawns, *ikan bilis* and clams wear off their juices into the stock. The eggs are scrambled into the bustling oil in the wok and transform from yellow liquid to a golden fluffy cloud, as it wraps around the egg noodles and white rice vermicelli (*'mi fen'*). The stock and noodles and seafood rise together in a symphonic movement and end in a plate garnished with chives and chilli and lime.

Because the chef worked the ingredients and utensils, there is a plate of *hokkien mee*. Out of chaos came order that was good, good at least to the eyes and the ears and the nose and to the tongue.

The chef said, "*let there be hokkien mee*", and so there was.

And the plate of *hokkien mee* will feed a hungry taxi driver who had just driven around Singapore for 12 hours without rest, or a doctor who's been seeing coughing and sneezing patients in the heartland clinic all morning, or the pastor who's just visited a sick elderly member nearby.

And it was good. The *hokkien mee* was good.

This Word that lit the universe is the Word who beckons you into the warmth of His being.

So open up and let the Word of God light your world.

Let the Word of God shine on you just as God spoke light into the dark universe.

Let the Word of God light the darkness in your heart, examine every vein and chamber, and do surgery on where it's needed.

Let the Word of God light the darkness in your doubts.

Let the Word of God light the winding paths you are wandering on: His Word is a lamp unto your feet, a light for your path.

So don't trust in your own reason, but trust in Jesus the divine wisdom, and the very reason for who you are, who you were and who you will be.

Let the Word of God light your world.

Here, then, is a suggestion. The next time you are about to undertake a chore, reflect on how the work you're about to do reflects the work of God, in bringing order and light.

Meditate on the work of God, on *a specific work* of God, as you go about the task. Let the thought unravel in your heart as your hands revel in the work.

Or consider how your act of service will bring some clarity and light into someone else's life, thoughts, or heart. Even if it is just writing that one email. Or uttering that one prayer.

Who knows that perhaps through that, the light of the world will illumine your inner world.

To Work and Keep all that God has made

There is a fundamental difference between God's work of creation and human work. God *created out of nothing*. And *God recreates*. We humans cannot create from nothing. We can only take what God created and work it. We can only *keep* and steward the things He's made.

Consider the first Garden at Eden. Adam and Eve did not create a single tree or flower or animal or bird or drop of water in the river.

God created all these things and then when everything has been prepared, God set humanity there. Like parents who prepare their home—with a comfortable cot, and a diaper changing station, and blackout curtains for good sleep, and cute animal prints on the walls—for their new-born baby.

So it is with God. The Father planted every fig tree in its place, unfolded the petals of every carnation, and stirred the spring water to rise from deep beneath the earth. And then the Father breathed life into His children and placed them there in the garden to work it and keep it.

"The LORD God took the man and put him in the garden of Eden *to work it and keep it*": Genesis 2:15.

Humanity's purpose is to work and keep the garden of this world.

The word "keep" here is "*shamar*" in Hebrew, which means to care for, to tend to, to steward, to obey, to cherish, to store up, to watch, to protect, and to celebrate.

The angular leaves like dancers with fans from the tree Adam might have named "*eh-der*", which we name maple trees, that turn brown and pirouette in the air and then land on the grass bed: these must be gathered leaf by leaf.

The wee lamb with barely a tuft of white wool on his head, whom Adam might have named "*ha'eynayim hagedolott*" (meaning 'big eyes'), Adam had to guide him to the gentle river to lap up the cool water. This too is work.

God created. We do not create. **We work and keep what God has created.**

And in that sense, every object of our work is precious. You are not dealing with merely your employer's goods. You are dealing with things that were manufactured from things that were ultimately created by God Himself.

Even the pieces of A4 paper you use to scribble meeting notes or print invoices on are derived ultimately from living breathing trees that no human created.

Even the dull metallic computer you use in your office is made up of materials that are derived ultimately from elements God designed.

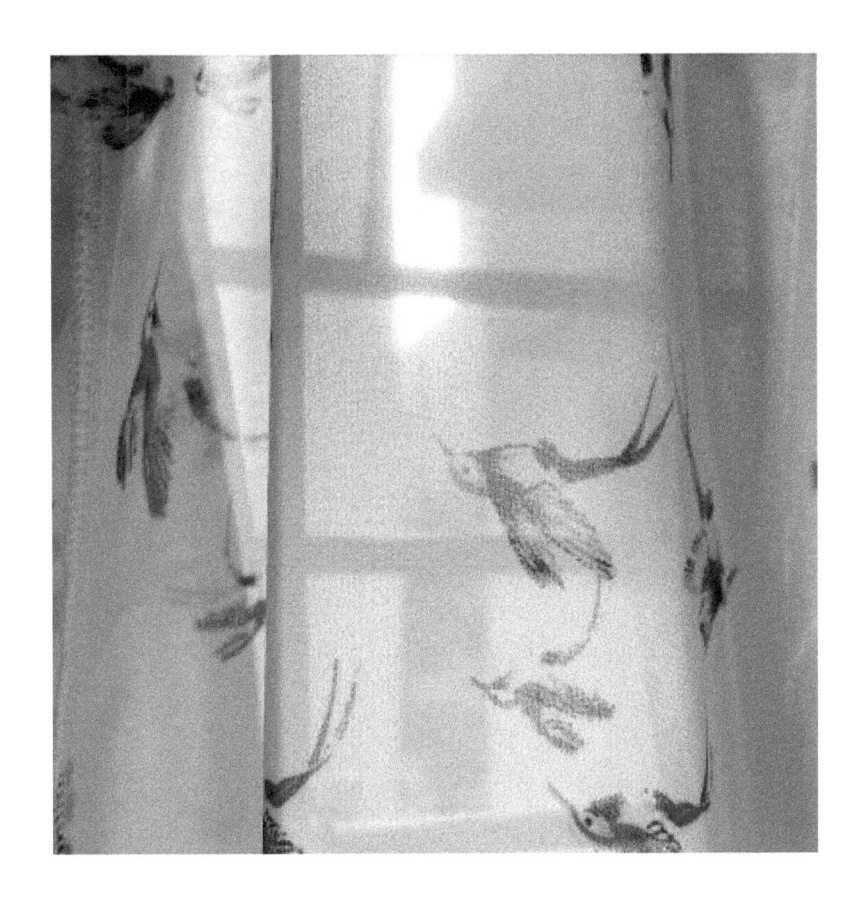

SO, WE CANNOT TAKE any of our work lightly. When we work, we are handling the very things God has made and has given to us to work and keep.

And so, we treat our environment—all of Creation with its manifold living creatures and non-living monuments and elements—most delicately. They are not our creation, but God's creation. They are not our work, but God's handiwork. We cannot go into an artist's home and throw rubbish at his artwork or set them on fire or leave them to wear away by neglect. What more if this artist is someone we profess great love and respect for?

And yet, we cannot forget the pinnacle of Creation, the high watermark of beauty, the most wonderful and awe-inducing work of God: Adam and Eve. In the image of God Himself, God created people. His very breath is breathed into us.

YES, THE STRANGER WHO bumped into you in the lift is also one of the greatest masterpieces of God.

It's easy to marvel at the human beings we love. When we are infatuated with a crush like a pubescent teenager, or madly in love with our newly wed spouse, or just laid eyes on our new-born baby, it would be easy to love the person as a delicate masterpiece of God.

Yet, the irritating colleague at work who won't stop talking about himself, the domineering boss who smells like garlic, the persistently unreasonable client whose name you won't speak—these too are the hand-crafted masterpieces of God.

In Genesis 3:17-19, we learn that work has been cursed because of the Fall. One effect of the curse is described as the "thorn and thistles". A thistle is a flowering plant with sharp prickles all over it. Think of all the foregoing possible persons who may cause you grief. These are your thistles. *The thorn and thistles in our lives are also God's masterpieces.* What shall we do with them? Still, we must work and keep with care and diligence. They are not ours but God's.

I think of John, whom I mentioned at the start of the book. I must conclude that somehow, even if it seems like the outcome appears insignificant, the presence of my team member and myself with him during that short time of his journey through his crisis, and tending to his matter and more importantly, tending to his soul, mattered. It mattered because it is simply doing the very thing we ought to do–through the work of our hands, to tend to a person whom God has made.

I think of Kay and her partner. Sometime after my wife and I hosted Kay in our home, Kay's partner got into trouble with the law. I took on the case pro bono and through the process, got to interact with him as an individual person. Not a mere reference in a conversation. My team and I advocated for him and argued for an appropriately (lesser) sentence than what the prosecution sought. He was eventually convicted and sentenced accordingly. Later, my friend and ministry partner updated that after he came out of prison, he started drinking alcohol again and one day brought Kay to a hotel. There, something terrible happened and he beat her so badly that one of her ribs fractured. Eventually, Kay separated from him for good and obtained a protection order for herself and her children against him. Since then, Kay has been working on rebuilding her life, caring for her children, and slowly working on her alcohol addiction to reduce the amount she drinks. The ex-partner separately is on a journey of finding a firmer footing for his life. Last, he was considering working towards becoming a fitness instructor.

The thing about working with people, and tending to those whom God has made, is that there are no Hollywood-type happy endings. Every season is a new chapter. A slow trudge sometimes through muddy waters, and sometimes on pleasant pasture. But it never ends. And so, still, we just keep on. And tend to what has been given to us in that moment.

Sometimes, I take some time out to visit elderly individuals from my church community, or relatives, or relatives of friends, who are living alone in nursing homes or community hospitals. I go into a bland space surrounded by many bars and grilles, and find them lying droopy on their bed. They take a while to recognise me. I greet them, ask how they are, offer to read a Psalm or two, sing a hymn, and pray with them. Sometimes I bring my young child hoping perhaps they would spark joy. There would be none. Even if there is any, it is not displayed as we would imagine it would be. No achievements to shout about. No social-media worthy photos to be posted. Nothing to spin into a LinkedIn post about being 'humbled' or 'thrilled' to have done anything at all. It is just the task of tending to one person for one brief moment.

I'm reminded of a programme called No One Dies Alone (Noda) with Assisi Hospice. Volunteers would take turns to sit at the bedside of a dying person who has no family or friends to be with them in their final hours. A volunteer recounted how a nurse 'grabbed' her and led her to sit by a dying patient the first time. She sat beside him for 3 hours and held his hand until he passed away.[12]

A cynic might say that such work does almost absolutely no good for the betterment of the world and has almost zero impact. After all, the recipients of such efforts are already moments away from their death.

However, we could shift our perspective and recognise it to be a declarative act. That even the dying has immeasurable value. And somehow this becomes a transformative act. It confronts our society's value system of treating people transactionally based on their usefulness. People matter just because they're human. Humans loved by a God who vested His image in them. And I would imagine that from the Maker's perspective, God would be pleased with these volunteers who tend to His own.

I'm reminded of a time at work when in what must be a God-orchestrated way, I got involved in two separate matters concurrently which left a deep impression on me. One involved a child at an international school, and another a migrant worker.

The child's parents were embroiled in a dispute and had effectively abandoned the child. The mother, I was told, last spoke to the child saying that she was not going to care for him any further. The father was absent. The child's grandparent however would like to care for him but doesn't know how to take him out of Singapore and take over legal authority to become the guardian of the child. The school's teachers and staff stepped in and went beyond their call of duty, as it were, to find ways to help the child and the grandparent. That included reaching out to seek my advice on the legal aspects of the situation. I say beyond the call of duty because really, the child was effectively no longer a student at the school. Who knew if school fees were even still being paid.

In the other case, the migrant worker suffered a severe medical condition. He needed a particular costly medical treatment, which the insurance policy could not possibly cover. The doctors, medical social workers, and other staff went above and beyond to figure viable solutions to arrange for him to be medically repatriated to his home country and receive the treatment back home where it would be cheaper. They reached out to me to seek legal advice on certain issues. These hospital professionals were, I'm sure, busy with many other cases. They had done their part in rendering the right diagnosis and advice and could have simply left it at that if the patient was unable to afford medical care. Technically, the employer also had fulfilled their responsibility. But every person involved went further to make the way possible to do what is best for the migrant worker.

I don't know why, but in my meetings with these two groups of dedicated workers who went the extra mile, I was so moved I teared up. Their selfless service inspired me and reminded me of the holy vocation of work—to tend to and keep those which God has made.

Perhaps it would serve you to practise this into truth: at the beginning of each day, begin your workday with this petition to God: *Lord, with the work of my hands, help me to tend to and keep those you have made.*

At the end of each day, run through the day's events and ask God to show you how there's at least one thing you've done which went towards tending to and keeping what God has made.

And then give thanks to the Lord for that. For this too is a gift—to be able to fulfil your high calling of work.

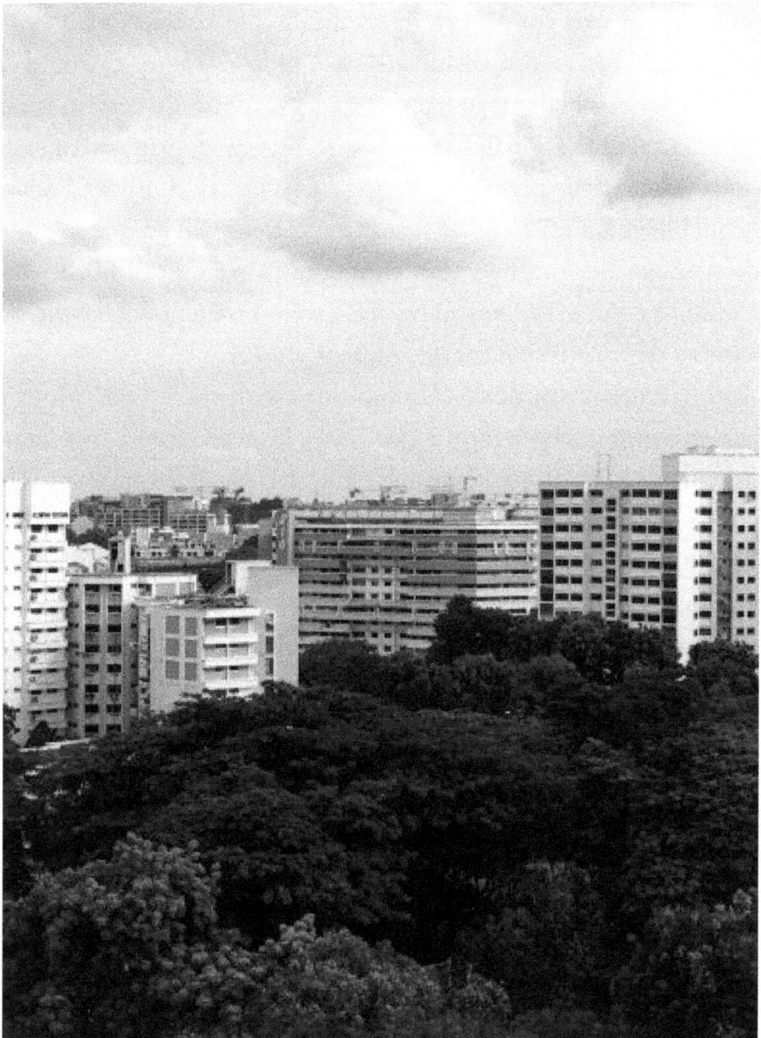

Keeping the Word Matters

To keep what God has made speaks also to keeping another treasure from God. It stems from a double meaning in Genesis 2:15-17:

> "15 The LORD God took the man and put him in the garden of Eden *to work it and keep it*. 16 And the LORD God *commanded* the man, saying, 'You may surely eat of every tree of the garden, 17 but of the tree of the knowledge of good and evil you shall not eat, for in the day that you eat of it you shall surely die.'"

Immediately after it was said God put Adam in the garden to work and keep the garden, God commanded Adam.

It appears that the work God gave to Adam was not merely watering the sunflowers or trimming sheep's wool. The work that God gave to Adam was to **keep God's command**.

Keep the garden. And keep your word to **keep God's word**.

How difficult could it be? The command was easy. You can eat from every tree in the garden—goodness knows how many trees there were! Maybe hundreds? Maybe thousands?—but don't eat from just that *one* tree.

Adam could not keep that one command. It was just one command! To not eat from just that one tree!

Adam failed in his work. And so, he was banished from the garden.

But because he failed in this work, he also made work difficult for all his descendants, including you and me.

Genesis 3:17-19:

> "17 ... Cursed is the ground because of you;
> through painful toil you will eat food from it
> all the days of your life.
> 18 It will produce thorns and thistles for you,
> and you will eat the plants of the field.
> 19 By the sweat of your brow
> you will eat your food
> until you return to the ground,
> since from it you were taken;
> for dust you are
> and to dust you will return."

And so it is with our work today. Whatever work we do, we are bound to experience the painful toil, the sweat of the brow, the thorns and thistles.

STILL, THEN, WE MUST work. Because work is what God has purposed us to do.

And work is the God-given way by which we will gather our food to feed ourselves and our families.

But work is not only for food. Just as Man shall not live on bread alone but by every word that comes from the mouth of God (Matthew 4:4), our work is not only so that we can buy the bread we feed on.

Our greater work is to live by the word of God.

The word of God that was spoken in the beginning at creation.

The word of God that came from the mouth of God, and by which awesome beautiful things was spoken into existence, like the Andromeda and the Pleiades, and the 79 moons of Jupiter and the ice cool rings of Saturn, and the powerful Gullfoss waterfall in Iceland, and the unbroken lines of the Himalayan mountain ridges, and the Amazon river.

The word of God that is revealed over thousands of years to the people of God.

The word of God memorised and retold orally and passed from generation to generation.

The word of God painstakingly written down by dedicated scribes on scrolls and parchment.

The word of God that points us to the very embodied living and breathing and walking Word of God, the Logos, Jesus Christ.

The word of God that calls you to the work of believing in the One whom God has sent (John 6:29).

Our greatest work is to live by the word of God, to believe in the Word of God, Jesus Christ.

DOES ANYTHING MATTER? WHY A CHRISTIAN SHOULD STILL CARE IN A WORLD OF DESPAIR

The Work We Create Matters

And yet, the amazing thing is that this work given to us by God, this work which may seem so incomprehensibly and unfathomably overwhelming, is itself a gift.

This work is grace.

This work is to rest in Jesus. Because to believe in Jesus is not only work. To believe in Jesus is to rest in Jesus. To believe in Jesus is to let ourselves be opened up, dissected, before Him for Him to re-create us.

God created us. God is re-creating us.

That's what recreation is. God is re-creating us from the inside out.

When we do the greater work of living by God's word, God speaks His word into our souls and re-creates us and remakes us anew.

Frederick Buechner says in Alphabet of Grace:[13]

> "Darkness was upon the face of the deep, and God said, "Let there be light." Darkness laps at my sleeping face like a tide, and God says, "Let there be Buechner." Why not? Out of the primeval chaos of sleep he calls me to be a life again. Out of the labyrinth of cells, born and unborn, remembered and forgotten, he calls me to be a self again, a single true and whole self. He calls me to be this rather than that; he calls me to be here rather than there; he calls me to be now rather than then. He calls me to be of all things me as this morning when the alarm went off or the children came in or your dream woke you, he called you to be of all things

you. To wake up is to be given back your life again. To wake up—and I suspect that you have a choice always, to wake or not to wake—is to be given back the world again and of all possible worlds this world, this earth rich with the bodies of the dead as our dreams are rich with their ghosts, this earth that we have seen hanging in space, our toy, our tomb, our precious jewel, our hope and our despair and our heart's delight. Waking into the new day, we are all of us Adam on the morning of creation, and the world is ours to name. *Out of many fragments we are called to put back together a self again."*

"Let there be light," God spoke.

In your heart, God speaks, "let there be light" and this light is the life of Man. This light sets your heart ablaze with the very life of the cosmos, the breath of God. And darkness shall not overcome it.

And every time we lay ourselves bare before God, every time we make that choice in our heart to walk by the word of God, we let God speak His word into our souls to bring light and life, to remake us, to recreate us, and we are slowly being made new, we are slowly being reshaped into the handcrafted masterpiece God has in mind.

Michelangelo said "The sculpture is already complete within the marble block, before I start my work. It is already there; I just have to chisel away the superfluous material."

God, the master artist, sees that masterpiece in you. It is already there. He just has to chisel away the superfluous material.

"For we are God's *masterpiece*. He has *created us anew* in Christ Jesus, so we can *do the good things* he planned for us long ago." Ephesians 2:10 (NLT).

And so this is the amazing work that's happened and that's still happening now: the God of beginnings, the God in time and outside time, the God of the seasons—this God created you; He is creating you anew in Christ Jesus; He purposed you to work and to keep the garden of this world and to keep His word; He purposes you to do good work. As you keep His word, the Word of God, the Logos of God will be spoken into your soul, and you will be re-created anew to do good work.

You are God's masterpiece created and recreated by His Word to create beautiful masterpieces in the garden of His world.

So go forth into the world and keep God's world with care; live His Word; do good works; and make beautiful things.

Does Loving Your Neighbour Matter?

To keep the work of God is to keep the word of God.
   Love is the word we are to keep.
The two Greatest Commandments, Jesus says, is to love.
Love God wholly and love our neighbour rightly.
These two commands we are to keep are intertwined. That is, to love God is to love neighbour; to love neighbour is to love God (1 John 4).
The difficult question, however, is what does it mean to love? To love neighbour? To love God?
The definitional question is the threshold question. The line in the sand that defines what we must do and what we are free from obligation of. And we won't be the first to ask this question.
We consider Luke 10:25-37.

Who is your neighbour?

Who is my neighbour? The question was first asked by a lawyer, such as yours truly, to justify himself. Justify means to be satisfied as just. The lawyer wanted to satisfy himself that he was just. To ask the definitional question is the fundamental tool in every lawyer's playbook.

Jaffa cakes. Are they cakes or biscuits? In the United Kingdom, McVities brought a legal dispute to the courts to argue that Jaffa cakes are not biscuits, but cakes. This was so that McVities would not be charged full Value Added Tax (VAT) on it. McVities' lawyer's decisive argument was that cakes harden when they go stale, whereas biscuits become soggy. Jaffa cakes harden. McVities even produced a giant Jaffa cake in court to illustrate the argument that it's actually a cake not a biscuit! Eventually, McVities won.

The lawyer in Luke 10 similarly argued definitions. He wanted to limit the definition of "neighbour" so that he could justify, or satisfy himself that he's just, by the two Greatest Commandments of the Mosaic Law.

What was he likely thinking? It's very easy to satisfy the law if "neighbour" means *only* the people that are easy to love anyway. E.g. his family members, his mates. When asked, "have you loved your neighbour?", his answer would surely be a resounding yes.

Jesus knew very well what the lawyer was doing. After telling the parable, Jesus turned the tables and asked the lawyer: "who *proved to be a neighbour* to the man who was robbed?"

The lawyer did not even want to say the word "Samaritan". So, he had to say, "the one who showed him mercy".

In this move, Jesus challenges our definition of neighbour. The question should not be "who is my neighbour?" but **"who can I be a neighbour to?"**

The parable suggests that **there is no limit to the definition of neighbour.** The person you encounter on the street. What is their ethnicity? What is their religion? What is their occupation? Which political party do they vote for? What is their social-economic status? Are they a Liverpool or Man United or Arsenal supporter?

So, in this parable, I think Jesus is saying that **a neighbour is anyone you can *potentially* be a neighbour to.**

I know it's circular and self-referential. But that's what Jesus does with us. Turns our attempts to self-rationalise into self-searching. The focus of this definition is not on others but on ourselves.

Who am I a neighbour to?

Who can I be a neighbour to?

Will you be a neighbour? Between compassion and diversion

" Now by chance a priest was going down that road, and when he saw him **he passed by on the other side**": Luke 10:31.

Why did Jesus say, "by chance"? I think it was to emphasise that the neighbour relationship is not what we choose or plan beforehand.

The fact that a person is a neighbour is determined by God. The only choice we have is to accept or deny the person as a neighbour. It is like a sibling. You don't get to choose your sibling. You can choose to love or deny the person as your sibling.

In this parable, by chance, an opportunity to become a neighbour arose; by chance, a choice to love or deny a neighbour; by chance, a moment to choose.

But is any such moment really *chance*? Does the material universe really just exist on a string of dice throwing? Or is such a moment destined by God?

The priest and the Levite saw the man and could have chosen to accept the victim as a neighbour. They could have chosen to *love* the victim as a neighbour.

Or they could have chosen to *deny* him as a neighbour.

The priest and Levite would likely have thought: oh, that could be an injured man or a dead body; if it's a dead body, I'd better steer far away from it or else I'd be defiled—(but they were heading to Jericho from Jerusalem so they would have finished their temple duties; even if they were to become ceremonially unclean (Numbers 19:11-13), they would have to just wait 7 days (1 Chronicles 9:25) and go through a ritual cleansing process; their duties were in one-week cycles; and there would have been quite a number of divisions, so their next rostered duty slot would have been after the 7 days).

Or maybe they thought: oh, I should see if it's an injured man who needs help? But if it's an injured man, that would be a lot of inconvenience for me. I'm heading home to Jericho after my tiring religious duties in Jerusalem. I just want to go back and sleep.

Whatever it is that ultimately made their decision, they *saw* the man and *chose* to pass by the man **on the other side** of the road.

The Samaritan saw the same man. What happened? Jesus said he felt **compassion**.

Compassion here means to be moved. The Greek word is "*splagchnizomai*". Strong's dictionary explains the word as follows: "*to be moved as to one's bowels, hence to be moved with compassion, have compassion (for the bowels were thought to be the seat of love and pity)*". Strange, we modern people think the seat of love is the heart. People in the past thought love is to have a *lao sai* (diarrhoea) feeling. Much more visceral, isn't it?

Compassion is to be gripped by a strong emotion of care for a person.

Now, at this point when Jesus is telling this parable, you would expect the lawyer and the Jewish crowd to gasp or feel a burning fury rise within them. The Jews hated the Samaritans. For us, it may be hard to imagine the disgust the Jews would have had for the Samaritans. These days, there is no analogy which we can publish which is not politically incorrect, even if the reality of racial hatred is still experienced by many all over the world.

The implication suggested in the parable is that the pious priest and Levite were heartless, whereas the Samaritan had a heart.

And because the Samaritan had a heart, he proved himself to be a neighbour. The challenge Jesus poses to His Jewish audience would be: would you love *this* neighbour? A Samaritan.

The Samaritan saw the injured man and **chose compassion, not diversion**.

Saw and chose to see him as a neighbour, not a burden.

Saw and chose to love him as a neighbour, not deny him.

What about us?

Many of us go to church weekly, sing worship songs, serve dutifully, give of our time and treasures, teach the Bible, and the moment we step outside church, we leave our Jerusalem and embark on the road to our Jericho.

On this road to Jericho, we will certainly encounter a neighbour.

THINK NOW OF THE PEOPLE you encounter on a daily, weekly, monthly, or yearly basis. Imagine yourself fast forwarding your past week or month. Think of the places you walk through or inhabit, the communities you are a part of. Your home and family, your next-door neighbours, your school, your bunk and platoon mates, your work colleagues, the hawkers you buy your lunch from, the labourers you walk by, your church and church neighbourhood, your friends you play football with or catch up with from time to time at a hipster cafe over a latte.

Who comes to mind? What faces do you see? Who are these people?

Would you see, as I see in my mind's eye, the Indian gentleman Mr. Clifford who enunciates his words like a fresh jotter book, living alone on the 11th floor whose brother's family lives in Sydney and whose mother had dementia.

Or Mr. Ang, with his balding patch covered by shy wisps of hair, who has had an eye condition and whose hearing is weakening, whose wife had kidney failure and whose life savings were spent on medical care for her.

Or the middle-aged lady Janice who told us how fragile life is, and how her toddler grandson's classmate suddenly passed away from some sickness.

Or the elderly freckled Mdm. Ng who smiles kindly as the wrinkles at her eyelids crease together like a cracked Mandarin orange and who pours out her life story to us in Cantonese even though we could not understand a word of it and we could only nod and smile back?

(These are the neighbours in a block of one-room flats near my church that my then church small group visited several times a year.)

Would you see, as I see, the middle-aged man B who has been staying at our church's homeless shelter and who proudly shared about the skills he learnt and still remembers from St John's when he was in Secondary School.

Or the migrant worker pro bono client who was cheated of his savings whom I acted for, with whom I had dinner where we talked about our families and lives, and who bought me matcha ice cream in gratitude.

Or the friend, whose mother was in Intensive Care Unit (ICU) battling cancer, whom a friend and I visited at the hospital?

Who do you see?

Will you choose to see the person **as a neighbour or burden?**

Will you see and **choose compassion or diversion?**

See and choose to **love or deny a neighbour?**

Will you choose to walk *towards* the person or walk on the *other side of the road?*

Which side will you walk?

Every such moment we find ourselves in is a moment destined by God. A moment of testing. A moment for us to choose.

Every person we encounter is a neighbour God has placed in our life.

We can choose to look away, but we can never say we did not know. That's a quote from William Wilberforce.

We could also add, we can never say God does not know that we chose to look away.

That is why Jesus turns the question "who is my neighbour?" to the real question.

And the real question is **"how can I be a neighbour?"**

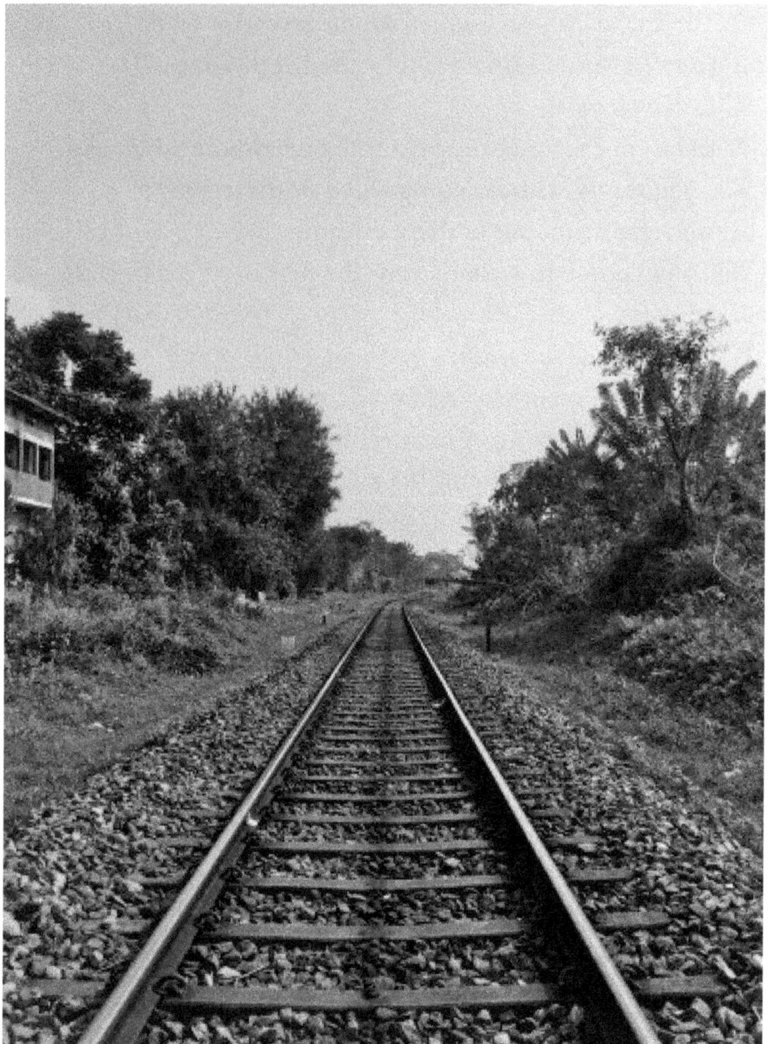

How Can You Be a Neighbour?

How then can we be neighbours?

Being neighbours does not only mean showing mercy, just because the lawyer in the story used the word "mercy". We should be careful not to import our ideas of mercy and love into the great commandments.

When I say the word "mercy", our modern association of the word is to grant pardon for some punishment. But mercy does not only mean that.

Neither is mercy the only way to love a neighbour.

Neither are our ideas of love—as romantic or sexual—appropriate.

That the word to love God and love neighbour are intertwined means that the shape of love is marked by the shape of God's heart.

It's curious that we often bandy about the phrase love your neighbour in tandem with only this Parable of the Good Samaritan. Very few people talk about the passage in the Old Testament that this phrase came from. There seems to be only one Old Testament passage where this phrase comes from.

And that is Leviticus 19. The passage, as it seems to me, embodies the two Greatest Commandments: love God and love neighbour.

It's interesting that the commands in verses 9 to 18 that culminate into the "love your neighbour" command are varied.

- Gleaning principle: leave some profit margin for the poor or needy migrant to glean for themselves.

- Speak truth to one another.
- Be kind to the weaker members of your community.
- Be fair in your dealings with one another.
- Be impartial in making judgement.
- Don't slander or gossip or stir trouble.
- Don't hate or bear a grudge or take vengeance, but reason sincerely (or mediate and make peace) with people.

There is more to Leviticus 19, but I shall not set them all out here. The whole passage seems to me to revolve around the same themes. Social justice. Truth. Fairness. Peace-making. Holiness.

To sum it up with another biblical phrase: 'justice and righteousness'.

So, it appears that loving our neighbour is not always the grand noble act of rescuing a person from the throes of death.

It is also the unseen commitments to truth and peace we forge in the humdrum day-to-day.

It is also the small choices of what is good and right we make in the quotidian.

It is also the deliberate forbearance from venting our anger.

It is also the waiving of our entitlement to maximise profits and rights, leaving margin and opportunities for the vulnerable.

To love our neighbours, then, is not an emotional sentiment, but an act of will; to prefer greater things than our self-interests—greater things like justice, truth, fairness, peace, holiness, and the welfare of others; to search our hearts and minds, and to invite God to wash clean the grime there. All of which happens in the minutiae and quotidian of our everyday life.

In this sense, loving our neighbours does not have to be a practical and philosophical nightmare whereby every person we encounter forces us to stop or demands our attention and care. Because in theory, the whole world could be a neighbour and if we were to stop for everybody, we would never be able to move.

We can, however, make everyday choices of what is right and just.

And occasionally, God places people in our lives, and the Spirit pulls at our conscience to stop and attend to the one.

It is this string of invisible commitments we make that calibrate our life orientation to God's character and will, and as we make our pilgrimage through life following this life orientation, as we interact with a tangible world, the visible effects of the invisible manifest themselves. It is the interpersonal human embodiment of quantum entanglement. The constant hum of potentiality ready for transformation into that which matters, the means of divine grace breaking into the static and ordinary.

Nobody, I think, is born into this world with an inner orientation towards God or compassion. And we all have to begin in the invisible, the darkness where no one else but God sees. In the beginning, God calmed the chaos and created what was good by speaking forth the boundaries of night and day, water and sky, land and sea, and so on. We all have to begin by calming the chaos, and speaking a word that draws the boundaries of that commitment.

WHEN I FIRST ARRIVED in London for a job stint of a few months, I was confronted early on by the homeless men and women on the grimy grey streets of London, their ashen and scraggly faces staring at me with eyes that I could see through so deep into their empty hearts. My first instinct, as would many others, was to avert their gaze.

I tried but I failed. I tried to reject diversion. I tried to stop. But I only tried when the moment came. And every time the moment came, it was always at an inconvenient time when I was rushing from work to my next appointment, or from home to the theatre, or whatever it was my pleasure-seeking agenda demanded. So, I made the commitment beforehand. I committed to use cash to pay for things so that I could get loose change. I used digital payments all the time before that. But I committed to setting aside all those loose change in my jacket pocket. So it is always accessible. I had no excuse for inconvenience or inaccessibility or inexpediency. And then it became a habit. I always had loose change. Most homeless folks I saw, so long as I had loose change, I'd give the person and greet them and say God bless. If it were a Big Issue seller, I'd buy a copy of the magazine and thank him.

I'm aware this is vulnerable to accusations of tokenism, and I'm not going to try to justify myself. The point to illustrate is the need for a prior commitment, a plan of action, the formation of a rhythm or habit, courage, and perseverance to keep going on, and critical self-reflection to adapt.

It is the commitments we make that calibrate our life orientation toward compassion.

And these internal commitments demand a lot more from us than external niceties.

To love our neighbour is to live authentically.

To strip away the veneer of courtesy and don sincerity.

To admit our own failings as we are confronted by other people's failings.

To bite our tongue when we feel entitled to cursing.

To speak truth in grace when the truth could be otherwise devastating.

To refrain from unleashing a barrage of missiles even though we have a whole arsenal at our disposal.

To pour out from our alabaster jar even when it's broken and leaking.

To build good fences but keep the gate always open.

To quietly leave behind that extra change for the waiting worker.

To lift up our eyes from our navel or feet or phones and look out for the people around us as we walk down our paths in life.

To step into the shoes of the people who step on our feet and feel how heavy those shoes are.

To be a companion to people in their passion (an old word that means suffering). For the etymology of the word compassion is *compati*: meaning to share in the suffering of another person.

To choose compassion over diversion.

Mercy Matters

In reflecting on the calling to be a neighbour with compassion, I am confronted by the challenge of doing so with people who do not deserve my compassion or care.

Even as I wrote that sentence, I struggle to think of who would be deserving. Surely my child when he was but a new-born infant. But not when he's a defiant toddler having a meltdown over being denied a second bottle of sweetened drinks. I have had pro bono clients who tested my patience and were entirely ungrateful. Nothing at all like the romantic portrayals in films. In such instances, I just wanted out as soon as I could.

Then I am reminded of the account in John 5. Jesus goes to the pool at Bethesda, meaning the House of Mercy on a Sabbath day. He finds a man with a disability who has been there for 38 years. Jesus asks him if he wanted to be healed. You would expect the answer to be a resounding yes, or if he has been made cynical by despair, then perhaps a sarcastic yes. Instead, the man's answer was, no one helps him to get into the pool when the water is stirred up. The background to that is that it was believed that when the water was stirred up, it was an angel who did so and anyone who got into the water at that time would be healed. The man's response was a bitter one of blaming others.

Jesus then commands him to stand up, take his mat and walk. He does so and goes off. The Jewish religious leaders saw the man and confronted him for doing that, allegedly because it was breaking the Sabbath. The man's response was to shift the blame to the man who healed him—he did not know Jesus' identity then. Later, when the man encountered Jesus at the temple, Jesus warned him to sin no more, so that nothing worse may happen to him. It suggests that he suffered something, perhaps his disability, because of his own sin, though we do not know what the circumstances were. And to be clear, it does not imply any general principle that people always experience suffering because of their own sin; however, the converse is often true, in that one's sin leads to harmful consequences for oneself and others. The mention of this statement here in this story, however, seems to be that this man is himself to blame for his circumstances. But as we have seen, he's a man who blames everyone else but himself. After learning of Jesus' identity, he then goes to report to the Jewish religious leaders that it was Jesus who told him to break the Sabbath law.

Not only is the man a bitter ingrate, but he also even went out of the way to bring trouble upon the man he recognises to have miraculously healed him! When I read this story, I boiled with rage! I did not know why I was so angry at first. Was I angry on behalf of Jesus? Now, I think it's because I have encountered many such people in my life who have given me trouble despite my help. I am angry at all these people, represented by this man in John 5.

In the story, the Jewish religious leaders then persecute Jesus. His answer to them was, "My Father is working until now, and I am working." He then goes on a discourse about doing only what He sees the Heavenly Father does.

Here, I realise that Jesus was doing the work of mercy at a place called the House of Mercy, on the Sabbath no less, because mercy is the very nature and character of God. God's mercy cannot cease. There is no resting from God's work of mercy. Even for a man who far from deserves any mercy.

When I shared my reflections with my wife, and how angry I was reading it, she reminded me that we are that man.

It is only because God never ceased in His work of mercy, because God felt compassion for me and came down into the miry pit I was in to reach me, that I, a man who deserves no mercy, may experience His mercy.

It is this mercy that compels me to keep His word. His word to love mercy and undertake the work of mercy. This mercy, when I allow Him to recreate me, is reshaping me into His image—that the shape of my heart may be the shape of His.

No doubt, I struggle. And all that I've considered above does not take away the need to have healthy and safe boundaries, and to exercise wisdom and discernment in undertaking any work of mercy and in exercising compassion.

Yet, it is what the Spirit keeps reminding me of when I am tempted to look away, to choose diversion instead of compassion. We who have received great mercy love greatly (Luke 7:47).

After we sing the last hallelujah, after we say the last "Amen", after the preacher dismisses us with the benediction, as we step outside of our church sanctuaries, as we depart from our Jerusalem and head back to our Jericho, as we make our long pilgrimage home, which way will we go?

Will we undertake the ceaseless work of mercy even with those who do not deserve it?

Will we choose to love greatly?

I suppose that it is worth considering, as a means to let the Spirit of God remould us into vessels of such mercy, that we undertake a commitment of charitable service which leaves us with no discretion of whom we must serve or care for.

Commit, for instance, to visit an elderly person in a nursing home every month, whoever that person may be, however adorable or cantankerous. Or to pray for a different person in your workplace every day, even those you aren't familiar with or are annoyed by.

After all, we are the objects of God's commitment to a ceaseless work of mercy unto us. May it then help us ceaselessly know and share His mercy.

DOES ANYTHING MATTER? WHY A CHRISTIAN SHOULD STILL CARE IN A WORLD OF DESPAIR

What If You Care Too Much? A Paralysis of Despair

"*Today's despair is a poor chisel to carve out tomorrow's justice*".
- Martin Luther King Jr

Perhaps for you, your affliction is that you care too much. That you despair when you see your finitude in the face of the enormity of the problem confronting you. And then you become paralysed by despair. It may be a paralysis of action or of the soul. And to be clear, I am not talking about clinical depression, for which one should seek professional help and other means to treat.

13th century theologian Thomas Aquinas wrote in his work *Summa Theologica*, that hope, as a natural virtue, is the desire for a future, difficult, yet possible good. As a theological virtue, hope is located in the will towards the good. And the ultimate good is God Himself. Despair then is a vice of the will turning away from the good. One who despairs acknowledges that the thing hoped for is a good to be pursued but cannot be obtained because it is too difficult. Augustine of Hippo makes the same observations in his work, The City of God.[14]

Despair, on first glance, is a negative condition to be avoided. Yet, despair seems to be an ubiquitous spectre in many people's lives, at least at some season of life. 20th century French-Algerian existentialist philosopher Albert Camus wrote, "There is no love of life without

DOES ANYTHING MATTER? WHY A CHRISTIAN SHOULD STILL CARE IN A WORLD OF DESPAIR

despair of life". Despair is inescapable for those who partake in self-examination.

19th century German philosopher Frederich Nietzsche wrote, "if you gaze long enough into an abyss, the abyss will gaze back into you." If you were to stare at despair for a while, you'd probably feel trapped in helplessness. Yet, if you were to stare at despair long enough, it will begin to reveal what is hidden within you.

IT REVEALS QUESTIONS. Questions about what you truly desire, what you fear, what you believe, what your faith is in, and most importantly, who you are.

19th century Danish theologian and philosopher Søren Kierkegaard wrote extensively about existential despair in his book The Sickness Unto Death. To him, despair is that divergence between two selves. He wrote:

> "The self is a relation which relates to itself... A human being is a synthesis of the infinite and the finite, of the temporal and the eternal, of freedom and necessity... A synthesis is a relation between two terms. Looked at in this way a human being is not yet a self. ... Despair is the imbalance in a relation of synthesis, in a relation which relates to itself."

In other words, despair is what happens when your finite temporal self is at odds with your infinite eternal self. And everyone who has eternity in their hearts will at some point face despair because it is inevitable that they would be confronted by their finitude. Kierkegaard says that you have to press deeper into the despair and reconcile the self that is not yet with the self that is to be.

Yet, what does it mean to be journeying towards the infinite eternal self? Surely, it is not that you could become an all-powerful being capable of solving every problem? It would be delusional to believe that is an actual possibility. Such is the root of false unfounded optimism.

Instead, the root of true hope is in embracing the infinite and eternal. This calls us to reconcile our false despairing self with the self that is entrusted to a great power of possibility. The Christian thus looks to God. For God is infinite, eternal, and all powerful. The God of possibilities. The God who makes all things possible which humans deem impossible.

The problem with our finite self-embracing an infinite God is our inability to fully comprehend the infinite. "For my thoughts are not your thoughts, neither are your ways my ways, declares the LORD. For as the heavens are higher than the earth, so are my ways higher than your ways and my thoughts than your thoughts": Isaiah 55:8-9.

DOES ANYTHING MATTER? WHY A CHRISTIAN SHOULD STILL CARE IN A WORLD OF DESPAIR

PHILOSOPHERS SINCE ancient times have tried to grapple with the notion of infinity. Zeno of Elia in circa. 450 BC came up with the "arrow paradox". An arrow can never hit its target, in his paradox, because when it has travelled half the distance to its target, its remaining path can always be divided by half, and so on, an infinite number of times. ½. ¼. 1/16. 1/32... Hence, it is impossible for the arrow to reach its target in a finite time. Of course, we know this is not in fact reality. This was later solved by way of the geometric series. When n in the series tends to infinity, the sum tends to 1. The sum of an infinite number of numbers can tend to a finite number. This notion of infinity however cannot be appreciated by perceiving in the physical dimension. Instead, it can only be understood in the metaphysical unseen dimension.

So it is with hope, which is where the finite reaches out for the infinite. For "hope that is seen is not hope, for why does one still hope for what he sees?": Romans 8:24-25.

I'm reminded of the two disciples on the road to Emmaus in Luke 24:13-35, their faces downcast, probably drooping with despair, because they had seen Jesus die on the cross. Although they had later learnt that Jesus' tomb was empty, they remained despondent. It took an equally intellectual, relational, and spiritual encounter with Jesus Himself, for them to see beyond the physical, and thus have hope revived in the spiritual. In the prison of their physical perceptions, they could not fathom anything as impossible and infinite as the resurrection.

In that encounter with Jesus, the seed of eternity placed in their hearts took root and budded into hope. It was by gazing into the abyss of despair that they finally saw through it and encountered the first fruits of Resurrection. It was by Jesus descending into the abyss of death that He could conquer death and tear open a rift in our physical reality, allowing all of us a vista of, and a gateway to, the Resurrection. To the New Creation.

A group of scientists studied the Mediterranean Pillow coral over sixteen years and observed them at one point completely ravaged. Not a single sign of life at all. Yet, later somehow, certain coral colonies which were considered utterly dead started to show signs of life again. This happened with no human intervention. It is almost like a resurrection.[15]

Where human beings may see only death and impossibility, God sees infinite possibilities, and new life. "What no eye has seen, nor ear heard, nor the heart of man imagined, what God has prepared for those who love him": 1 Corinthians 2:9. The one who has hope sees beyond the physical. They are capable of sowing seeds of hope. Of making windows in otherwise grim prison walls to let the light in and open people's souls to vistas of possibilities.

Yet, the one who holds hope is fully aware of their finite limitations. They eschew a utopian pipe dream. Theologian Paul Tillich in his book *Theology of Peace* wrote, "the basis for genuine hope is that there is something present of that which is hoped for, as in the seed of something of the coming plant is present".

Every act of love done in faith becomes a seed of hope. We are sowers. We are reapers. But we are not God, who alone is the one that makes a seed burst open into new life. While some other seeds lay dormant, until the time that Creation is emancipated from all the burden of brokenness.

When hope is understood like this, it shapes a grounded outworking of the triad of noble Christian virtues: faith, hope and love. It is not a gargantuan world-sweeping faith. It is instead faith like a mustard seed. It is not a hope demonstrated by cosmic fireworks. It is instead a hope in sowing one small seed at a time. It is not love in the abstract. Not love for entire populations or species or planets. It is love in the particular.

It is this much love which we are called to give. It is probably as much care as we can possibly manage. British Anthropologist Robin Dunbar studied primate group sizes and brain sizes and extrapolated that generally, human beings can only manage up to 150 stable meaningful relationships. Not just 150 people whose names you know. But if you were to bump into them in the bar, you would be comfortable enough to sit and have a drink with. This became known as "Dunbar's number". Numerous studies since then have been published to either support this theory or to debunk it. Other studies suggest a higher number of about double that sum. The company behind the famous Gore-Tex brand coincidentally discovered that if more than 150 employees were working together in one building, many social problems occurred. The company therefore started making buildings with a maximum capacity of 150 employees. Social media companies and game developers have referred to this number in designing their platforms.

Whether or not Dunbar's number is indeed correct or scientifically supported, our lived experience will probably inform us that there really is a limit to how many people we can truly know and care about. Frankly, I'm not even sure I have 150 people in my contact list that I could comfortably call and ask to have a drink with anytime. The number probably shrinks significantly if the question is put another way: who can you call at 3am to seek help from if you're in a non-life-threatening emergency?

Consider also teacher-student ratios in early childhood education. Studies show that lower ratios have generally been associated with greater gains in children's receptive language, general knowledge, cooperative behaviour, and verbal initiations, and lower hostility and conflict.[16] We need not debate, for the present purposes, what an ideal ratio is. We need only imagine the difference between a class of one teacher to 30 pre-schoolers on one hand, and a class of one teacher to 5 pre-schoolers. There is simply a finite limit to a person's attentiveness and care.

In contemplating the power of the particular, I'm also reminded of how the former German Chancellor Angela Merkel, probably one of the greatest state leaders of our time, led her government to change course on their refugee policy (in particular what's known as the Dublin Regulation), letting potentially a million refugees from Syria, Afghanistan and Iraq in. This was in August 2015. What led to the change? Commentators point out that just a few weeks before, Merkel encountered a teenage Palestinian refugee girl Reem Sahwil at a televised school visit.[17] Sahwil told Merkel, "I don't know what my future looks like as long as I don't know if I can stay, I'd like to go to college. That is really a . . . goal I'd like to achieve." Merkel told the girl the political reality that it was simply not possible to let every asylum seeker or refugee into the country. Sahwil broke down into tears. Subsequently, Sahwil's family was allowed to stay on in Germany. And the government changed course to allow more refugees in. (Of course, there were many other factors at play, and Merkel had visited a refugee camp earlier on. This account is not a comment on the rightness of the policy choice, or the legacy of Merkel.) One girl had one chance to tell her story and share her hopes. Who knows, but that may have changed the course of history? It is almost like the story of Esther in the Bible. Our minds may compute the universal, but our hearts are seized by the particular. A singular face that represents a whole nation.

It is in embracing finitude that we can truly begin to practise the virtues of faith, hope and love. We embrace finitude not in itself, but in entrusting our finite selves to the infinite. It is this which unravels the otherwise impossible knot of despair which binds our hands and gags our tongues.

Yet, the person who stares only at their finitude and despair will never be able to see past them. It requires seeing their reality in a different dimension. An infinite one.

The Scriptures affirm this and present us with a raw and pastoral depiction of this struggle with despair. In Psalm 42, the psalmist cries out, soaked in his tears, mourning the oppression of his people. He feels like he is constantly buried under breaking waves upon waves.

YET, HE IS IN CONSTANT conversation with his soul, as well as his God.

"Why are you in despair, O my soul?" he calls out in v 5 and 11. This is perhaps what Kierkegaard alluded to. The psalmist is talking to his despairing self to reconcile with his eternal self. He has chosen not to listen solely to his despairing self. He has chosen instead to contend with his wearied soul. He asks his soul a question to examine what he holds on to. What does he trust in and yearn for that caused his despair?

The psalmist also asks God honestly, "I say to God, my rock: why have you forgotten me?" (v 9). Here lies a paradox of faith and hope. To be able to say in the same breath that God is God, the rock of your hope, while yet questioning if He has abandoned you is uniquely a Christian privilege. That our own saviour would cry out in the greatest moment of anguish the same woe, "my God why have you forsaken me?" (Psalm 22:1; Matthew 27:46), is the clear pass for us to be able to go to the Most High God with our brutal rawest feelings. God invites us to go to Him with our despair. Not lock ourselves in our prison of darkness.

The psalmist, in his destabilised potentially groundless condition, also reaches deep into his past, his recollection, his beliefs, to find something firm to ground himself in. In v 4, he recounts being with his community in worshipping God. In v 8, he calls to mind God's character.

Yet, the psalmist does not take a spiritual shortcut with his despair. He does not simply say, ok, I'll just bury this feeling of hopelessness and sing to God now. Instead, in v 11, he concludes by again speaking to his distressed soul to hope in God, and to urge his soul to worship God. But at that moment, he does not. It would be an unbearable cognitive dissonance otherwise. Instead, he ends tentatively by continuing the struggle with himself.

If you have struggled with despair, you are probably familiar with this. Like grief for the loss of a loved one, it does not go away. Maybe it never does. But it is in the continuous struggle with it that constitutes your very act of hope. It is hope the size of a mustard seed. It is the crack in the wall through which light comes in.

In "Wasteland", the band needtobreathe sings,
"*Yeah, in this wasteland where I'm livin'*
There is a crack in the door filled with light
And it's all that I need to get by".

It reminds me of the time I closed the curtains in my room. Something curious happened. On the ceiling adjacent to the curtains, I saw an image of the view downstairs outside my window. It took me a while to realise that because there was a small gap in the curtains, my room inadvertently became a pinhole camera.

An awesome thing happens when light finds its way through just a tiny hole in an otherwise dark space. This *camera obscura* phenomenon has intrigued thinkers and scientists since ancient times. E.g., the Chinese philosopher Mo Zi wrote in *Mojing* about it in the 5th century BC. Later, people used it to observe solar eclipses, study the nature of light, and aid them in making art. The essential element for all this scientific and artistic flourishing to happen is the singular small hole of light in darkness.

A single small hole of light in a dark space is all that's needed for imagining infinite possibilities.

Perhaps a single small seed of hope is all that's needed for the unfolding of the eternal into temporal.

Perhaps your choice to press on in the struggle with despair is the single act of hope that's needed for today. The seed for tomorrow's grace.

What is something that could help widen the pupils in your figurative eyes to see the sliver of light in the darkness?

Maybe the next time you're in paralysis, ensconce yourself in a dark room, but leave a slit in the window curtains, and observe how your eyes gradually attune themselves to let the little light in. Or take time out to catch the sunset from a picturesque spot.

Mutter a prayer as you do so, if you could muster the will for it: *Lord, let the crack of light be all I need to get by.*

DOES ANYTHING MATTER? WHY A CHRISTIAN SHOULD STILL CARE IN A WORLD OF DESPAIR

What Matters to Keep Us Going?

Here's a thought about light. Light is the basis for almost all life on earth. Indeed, through the cycles of life, decay and fossilisation, light is what makes possible almost all the fuel we use on earth. And the light that gives and enables life on earth does not come from within earth. It comes from the Sun, which is outside the earth. We cannot touch the Sun or even look at it. But by it, as C.S. Lewis famously wrote, "I see everything".

It's no wonder that the lyrical Gospel of John begins with a cosmic literary depiction of Jesus as the Word, and the light of the world that gives life. Like the Sun, Jesus, the Word of God and the light of life, tangibly and personally enters our world, which otherwise lies in suffocating darkness. He illuminates and gives life. But if he never came from beyond, then we would have remained buried lifeless. For we would never have been able to conjure up light and life from ash and dust.

In contemplating all that we've considered thus far, we may find ourselves dissatisfied. It may seem like the impetus for keeping the Word of God, for choosing the way of love, is simply the fact that God is who He is, and He has called us to keep His Word.

The Scriptures make clear, however, that the fuel for a Christian's hope to persevere in keeping God's Word is the Resurrection life that God in His mercy has rebirthed us to enter and enjoy (1 Peter 1:3-9). It is because Christ came from the beautiful, glorious realms and entered into the darkness of our grim windowless prison. Christ lived and

DOES ANYTHING MATTER? WHY A CHRISTIAN SHOULD STILL CARE IN A WORLD OF DESPAIR

illuminated our life. Christ died on the Cross for the forgiveness of our sins, that we may be reconciled to God. And Christ resurrected from death as the first fruits of the New Creation. And this has fulfilled everything necessary for us to enter into His resurrection life and be spiritually reborn into the New Creation. If not for Christ, we remain blind in spiritual darkness. If not for Christ, there is no resurrection life to speak of. If not for Christ, there is no New Creation to look forward to. If not for Christ, we come from ash and dust and to ash and dust we return, and there is nothing more but the cold lifeless depths of *Sheol*.

Then truly, everything would be futile. Because if there is no tomorrow, then why live today as if anything mattered? If there is no resurrection life after death, then why live sacrificially even unto death? If there is no New Creation, then why bother about the present Creation or the future generation? Species suicide would be the most rational choice.

How can humanity fashion any glimmer of hope out of the darkness and dust of this world? How can anyone see hope if everyone is equally blind? How can we live as if there is such a thing as eternal life, if we cannot know anything beyond death? We need something or someone who is from beyond death, darkness, despair and dust to come to lift us out of this existence. To give us a ray of hope.

THE CHRISTIAN WORKS to keep the Word of God not because she believes she is avoiding punishment–whether by way of karma or torment in some fiery hell or suffering in the next life on the wheel of reincarnation. After all, Christ has already taken away all the wages of sin for those who believe and follow Him.

Instead, the Christian works to keep the Word of God because having had a foretaste of the resurrection life in Christ, she wants all of it, and wants all of those around her to have it.

I grew up as a child eating and loving the simple cheese toast. Just a slice of highly processed Kraft cheese on plain white Gardenia bread. Once, when I was about 8 years old, I even went overboard and stacked so much cheese it overflowed and made a mess of the toaster oven. Fast forward to years later. One day, I watched the 2014 film "Chef". There's a scene in it where Jon Favreau makes a grilled cheese sandwich. One could see and hear on screen the sizzling of the grill, slicing of the crispy bread, the oozing medley of cheese, and the deep crunch of the son biting into the sandwich.

It was a life defining moment for me.

Since that moment, I've been on a quest to find the best grilled cheese sandwich. I've tried making it with various recipes. I've been to various cafes with specialty grilled cheese sandwiches in Singapore and abroad. Earlier this year, the topic came up in a chat with my colleague, and I found out that he too shared this passion. He mentioned a cafe which served, to him, what was the best grilled cheese sandwich he's ever had, but that it had closed or moved. Sometime later, he found that it's (re)open. So, we made a trek there together and partook in a fellowship meal of one of the best grilled cheese sandwiches I've ever had.

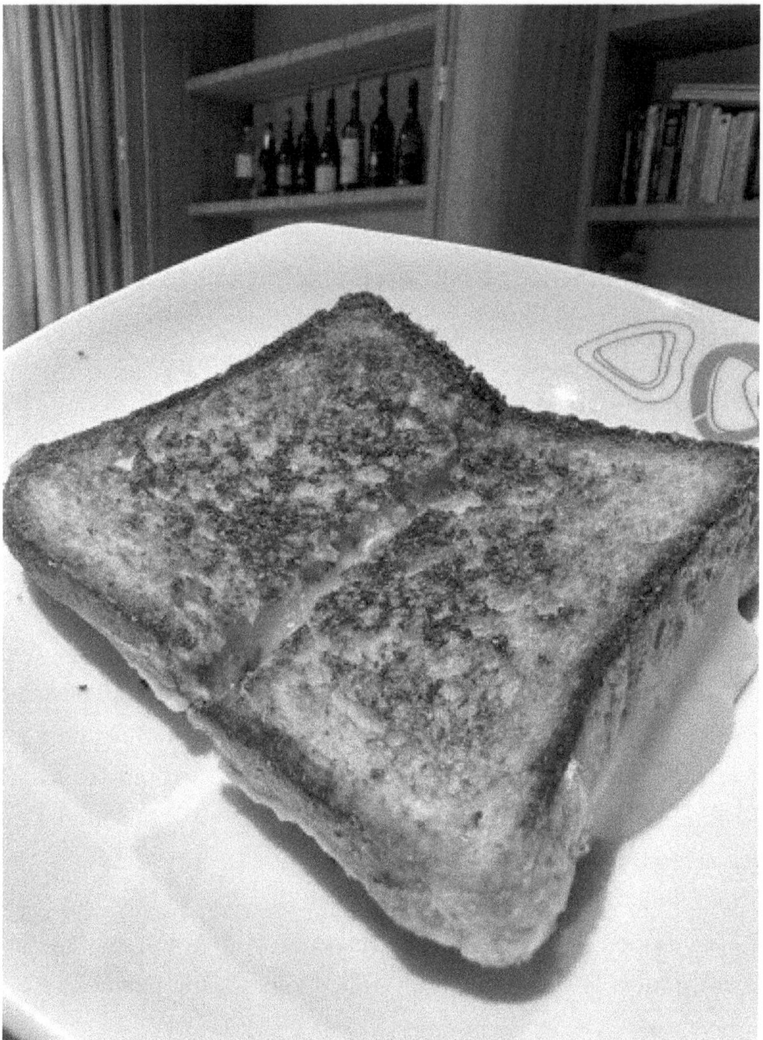

IN THE SAME WAY, WHEN the Christian does a small act of love unto the Lord, even if it does not bring complete healing or justice or resolution in this world, it is a foretaste of the New Creation for the person who experiences that love. It is like the on-screen depiction of a glorious grilled cheese sandwich. The person can't taste it or smell it or feel it. But they can see and hear it. And it is enough to possibly set them on a quest to search for the real thing. The best thing.

On that journey, there will be fellow pilgrims who enter their life and walk with them, pointing them in the direction of the good paths. (Of course, the Christian believes that in the first place, it is not the initiation of the person but of God that she could choose, begin, and complete the quest at all. That's a matter of the Spirit.)

It's not a coincidence that the Scriptures describe God, and life with and in God, in terms of food as well. Taste and see that the Lord is good (Psalm 34:8-10). Jesus declares Himself the bread of life (John 6:35). At the dawn of the New Creation, we will partake in the rich wedding feast of Christ (Revelation 19:7-9; Isaiah 25).

I grew up in a non-Christian family. In my teenage years, my soul was buried with depressive emotions and thoughts. In seeking to soothe it, I sought out all the wrong ways and means that were within reach; achievements, romance, sexual gratification, and more. After a long journey of wrestling with philosophical contentions and existential despair, I finally encountered Jesus and experienced His gentle life-giving salvific grace. Immediately thereafter, clichéd as it may sound, I felt like an entirely new being, transformed inside out. An overwhelming assuredness and security of who I am in Christ granted me a solid foundation of peace. And I wanted everyone around me to experience it too. It felt like the Holy Spirit was bubbling up a spring of life and I wanted to share it whenever I could. I wanted to tell everyone about the equivalent of the best grilled cheese sandwich.

There have been, are, and will be days where things of this world assault me and threaten to rob me of this peace. Days like these, I remember the supernatural peace I once had, and hold on with hope that one day, I will be wholly in Christ with endless days of peace.

The post-resurrection New Creation life is a life where the presence of God himself will cover us as a blanket of comfort, where there is no

DOES ANYTHING MATTER? WHY A CHRISTIAN SHOULD STILL CARE IN A WORLD OF DESPAIR

death or mourning or sickness or evil or suffering, where there will be healing of all hurts (Revelation 21:1-4, 22:1-5). And the light of life himself will be there.

In the meantime, the rare moments of enjoying a subliminal otherworldly experience of grilled cheese sandwich helps punctuate the long march of life with reminders of grace. And it is a gift enough to be filled with thankfulness.

One of my favourite movies is Shawshank Redemption. The movie centres on a banker named Andy Dufresne (Tim Robbins), who is sent to Shawshank Prison for life. He was wrongly convicted for murder. At the end of the film, Andy would successfully escape the prison after a legitimate opportunity for his conviction to be overturned was unjustly robbed of him. It would be revealed that Andy had been digging a tunnel in the prison walls for 20 years.

There's a scene in the film where Andy broke the prison rules and played a record of a Mozart aria "Le Nozze di Figaro" from the opera "The Marriage of Figaro" over the prison PA system. For a moment, in the grim hopeless prison, every prisoner stopped and became silent, and basked in the music, experiencing a moment of heaven. Andy was put into solitary confinement for this. After he was released, Red chided him and asked why he did it. Andy said, "There's something inside that they can't get to, that they can't touch. It's yours. Hope." Elsewhere in the film, Andy says, "hope is a good thing, maybe the best of things, and no good thing ever dies." The playing of the song represented a beautiful evocative reminder of the world outside beyond the prison. And that was the fuel for Andy's hope.

Everything that a Christian does faithfully unto God in the present life is a shadow of the post-resurrection New Creation life. Just like the Law and Prophets were a shadow of Christ, a witness to Christ, and a sign pointing to Christ. Every act of justice, mercy and love a Christian undertakes is a shadow, witness and sign pointing to the New Creation.

It is the bright song of hope that pierces the otherwise deafening silence of despair in the grim prison of this present world.

The Christian's work in the present life will be tested by divine fire, and rewards will be duly conferred (1 Corinthians 3:13-15). At the revealing of Christ and the whole of the New Creation, she will receive the fullness of grace and glory (1 Peter 1:13; Ephesians 1:18).

There is light at the end of the tunnel, and this light can be a captivating power for pressing on in the journey towards our ultimate home that lies beyond this present lifeworld (Philippians 3:13-14; 2 Corinthians 4:17-18).

So, what's the equivalent of your grilled cheese sandwich? And how have you sought to share that subliminal other-worldly experience with the people you journey with? Is there something in your daily vocation which points people to the divine or manifests a transient foretaste or image of the New Creation? Remember it again and again, with gratitude to God. And pray to be able to have more of such opportunities. Go forth and sow the seeds of hope near and far.

DOES ANYTHING MATTER? WHY A CHRISTIAN
SHOULD STILL CARE IN A WORLD OF DESPAIR

What Will All We Do Amount To?
Fruitfulness & Faithfulness

What Impact?

Many of us do what we do hoping to transform lives, impact society, and make the world a better place. Hoping that millions of people will come into the Kingdom of God or experience life transformation.

We slog, lead, serve, volunteer, mobilise, fundraise, strategize, plan, teach, equip, train, and sacrifice for the mission.

When the report card comes out, we look at the outcomes, numbers and statistics. Maybe the results are dismal. We feel like giving up.

Maybe it looks rosy. Yet, we wonder and doubt the real impact. Are lives transformed for the better? Are people experiencing the Kingdom of God?

And even if you're part of an organisation that has much to be proud of in terms of quantified impact, I'm sure you may have doubted yourself as an individual.

Have you ever felt like a lot of what you do is futile? Nothing matters? It will have no impact. Just doing the same thing again and again, and not seeing any results?

I've felt like this every so often. I'm sure you have. Perhaps about your work, your ministry, your family, your service, your spiritual life.

Don't we wish the things we do today could positively transform the whole wide world tomorrow?

And no matter how much strategizing, planning, forecasting, programming, it sometimes feels like we can never hit the right target.

John 15:1-17 (ESV):

"1 "I am the true vine, and my Father is the vinedresser. 2 Every branch in me that does not bear fruit he takes away, and every branch that does bear fruit he prunes, that it may bear more fruit. 3 Already you are clean because of the word that I have spoken to you. 4 Abide in me, and I in you. As the branch cannot bear fruit by itself, unless it abides in the vine, neither can you, unless you abide in me. 5 I am the vine; you are the branches. Whoever abides in me and I in him, he it is that bears much fruit, for apart from me you can do nothing. 6 If anyone does not abide in me he is thrown away like a branch and withers; and the branches are gathered, thrown into the fire, and burned. 7 If you abide in me, and my words abide in you, ask whatever you wish, and it will be done for you. 8 By this my Father is glorified, that you bear much fruit and so prove to be my disciples. 9 As the Father has loved me, so have I loved you. Abide in my love. 10 If you keep my commandments, you will abide in my love, just as I have kept my Father's commandments and abide in his love. 11 These things I have spoken to you, that my joy may be in you, and that your joy may be full.

12 "This is my commandment, that you love one another as I have loved you. 13 Greater love has no one than this, that someone lay down his life for his friends. 14 You are my friends if you do what I command you. 15 No longer do I call you servants, for the servant does not know what his master is doing; but I have called you friends, for all that I have heard from my Father I have made known to you. 16 You did not choose me, but I chose you and appointed you that you should go and bear fruit and that your fruit should abide, so that whatever you ask the Father in my name, he

may give it to you. 17 These things I command you, so that you will love one another."

Faithfulness brings Fruitfulness

Jesus left us instructions on this. For all that we do to bear fruit. John 15:4-5 says if we abide in Jesus, we will bear fruit. If we are faithful to Jesus, there will be fruitfulness.

Faithfulness brings fruitfulness.

How do we faithfully abide in Jesus?

First, v 10 says we are to keep Jesus' word / command. We have considered earlier what it means to "keep" the word of God. To obey, to live out, to cherish, to protect, to store up.

So, we must keep God's word in our heart and obey His word. We must tend to it in our soul regularly with great care, lest the weeds of the world fill up the soil and rob the good word of its place.

And God will prune us as we keep His word. When we let His word work in us, it will gradually scrub clean all the grime that is in our soul. That we may be healthy in spirit and capable of more fruit.

Second, we are to pray. V 7 says we are to pray for things we desire that's based on Jesus' word in our hearts. And God will do it for us so that we will bear much fruit, and He will be glorified.

Prayer is to call on our finite temporal selves to lift our gaze up to the infinite and eternal. To wrestle with our 'not yet' selves to reconcile with our 'to be' selves that God is recreating us into.

Prayer is to depend on God. Prayer is to shape ourselves into a posture of dependence on God. When we get on our knees, we curl up into that position of a foetus utterly dependent on the mother, a branch of the vine bending towards the sun.

Prayer is to press into our despair even when there is nothing visible or tangible that we can grasp as a sign of hope.

Prayer is to choose to continue the struggle with our despair although our circumstances suck all life out of us till we are but dry bones.

So, abiding in Jesus is to obey and pray.

We may think, let's come up with the strategy and plans and programmes to maximise our impact and fruitfulness. But this passage says, you can have all your strategies and plans, but if you don't abide in Jesus, you're not going to bear fruit.

Strategies and plans are important and necessary. But alone, they won't bring success. It's God who grows the fruit. It's abiding in Jesus that will bear fruit.

Your highly sophisticated computer with the top specifications can do amazing things like render 3D videos. Try sticking a tree branch into your computer. No matter how high tech it is, it's not going to make that tree branch grow fruit.

God is the vine dresser

And v 1 says God Himself is the vine dresser. He really wants to produce the best fruit for Himself. It is He who is zealous about fruitfulness and will do what it takes to produce the best fruit.

Because it will reveal us as Jesus' disciples. Because it will glorify Him.

So, let's not put ourselves ahead of God. It is His glory & His purposes that matter, that will ultimately succeed. Our job is to flow with His purposes. Abide in Him.

DOES ANYTHING MATTER? WHY A CHRISTIAN SHOULD STILL CARE IN A WORLD OF DESPAIR

Jesus is the true vine

And v 1 says Jesus is the true vine. We've got to be connected to the right vine to bear fruit. If you're a grape branch, don't get tied to a durian tree. You're just going to drop off and wither.

And if you're grafted to a root or vine that is destined to death and decay, then that too will be your end.

Here's an interesting fact worth a thought. Many of us are familiar with the prestige of top French and other Old-World wines. Some might even say they could be pretty snobbish about it. In the middle of the 19th century, French winemakers imported species of grapes from North America. Unfortunately, that brought along foreign aphids which caused a blight known as grape phylloxera. The Old-World wine grapes, unlike the American ones, were defenceless to this. Many of these vines were utterly wiped out. For two decades, vineyards across Europe were sucked out of life by these aphids. Because French grapes were exported to other winemaking regions where Old World vines had been used, these other regions, such as Australia, New Zealand, and South Africa, too were devastated.

Winemakers tried to battle the problem using strong insecticides and even flooding the vineyards. None were truly effective. The solution, as it turned out, after two decades of experimentation, was the age-old technique that the ancient world in biblical times would have been familiar with. Old World vines were grafted onto American roots which had developed resistance to the blight. Today, almost all wine grapes are grown from this American rootstock.

DOES ANYTHING MATTER? WHY A CHRISTIAN SHOULD STILL CARE IN A WORLD OF DESPAIR

The Scriptures similarly use the image of grafting into a spiritual source of life (Isaiah 60:21; Romans 6:4-6, 11:11-17). We who purport to follow Jesus are supposed to be grafted into the living vine that will not die. The danger is if we are grafted into a vine that, in the end, is susceptible to blight and decay. Sin entered the world through one man (grapevine?) and sin is overcome through one true Man (living rootstock?).

So, the question is: Do we really know Jesus? Are we living according to the true vine, Jesus? Or are we living according to our own beliefs, our own wisdom, or the philosophies and ideologies that's trending in the world right now?

So, **faithfulness brings fruitfulness.**

Faithfulness is to obey and pray.

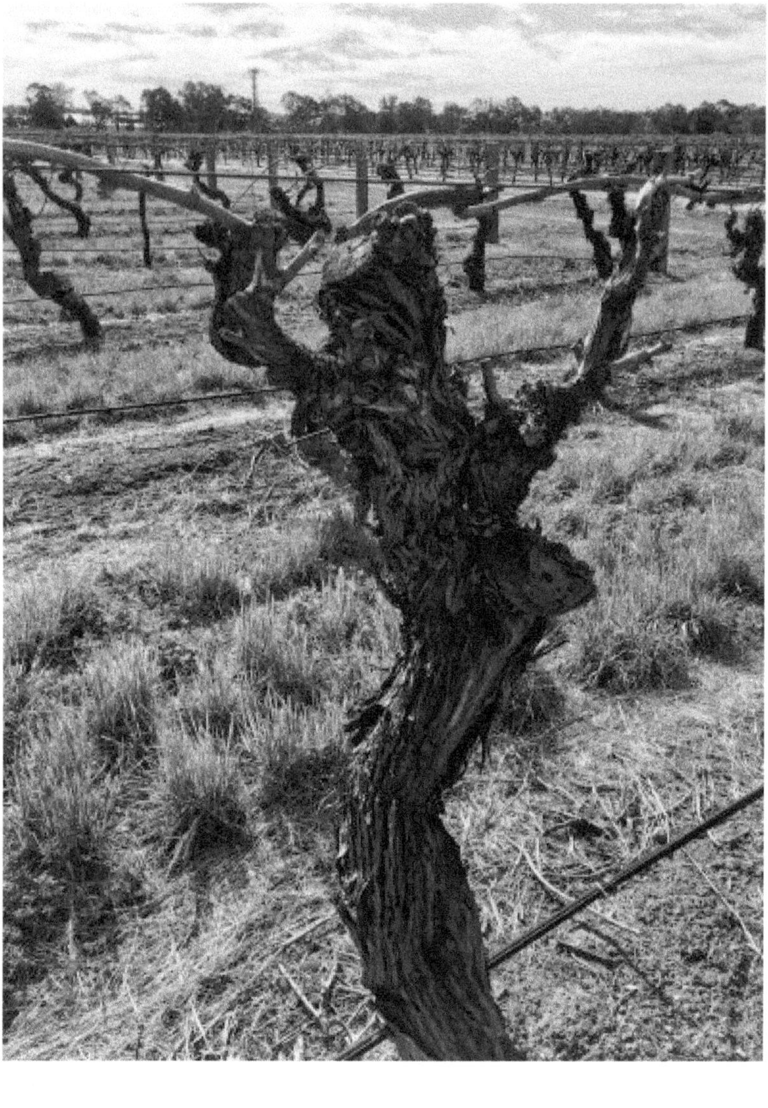

The command to obey

What is the command that we are to obey? V 12 reveals the command: love one another as Christ has loved us.

That is, to the point of sacrificing our lives. Not that we must die. But we must die to ourselves in loving one another. **Sacrificial love.**

This is Jesus' strategy. It's deceptively simple. But it worked.

This Jewish man (of course, not merely a man) with a small ragtag of followers turned the world upside down. With this one simple strategy. He loved His disciples even unto death. And He rose again. His disciples loved one another and Him even unto death. And their spiritual legacy flourishes today.

Scholars have recognised that the growth of the early church was not because of any strategy or personality.

It was instead because of this: they loved one another, they loved people, even unto the end of themselves. They sacrificed their wealth and comfort to care for the sick and poor among them. Even unto death. They rescued and redeemed slaves from slave ships. They cared for and buried those who were struck by plagues, when the world around them didn't dare to touch the sick and the dead for fear of themselves contracting the plague. They did this in faithfulness: in obedience to God's word and in prayer. They didn't know what fruit it would bring. But God used it to bear fruit.

So, **faithfulness brings fruitfulness. Faithfulness is prayer & obedience expressed in sacrificial love.**

God's orchestration towards fruitfulness

Sometimes, though, God encourages us by letting us have a peek at the fruit He's growing out of our little offering to Him.

I've been on an ongoing journey discovering what God is doing in terms of social justice, mercy ministry, and integral mission. I'm the National Coordinator of Micah Singapore, a community of Christians that are invested in these concerns.

Several years ago, I was helping with a homeless ministry. I got to befriend the founder of the ministry. He had been serving in this area for some time already, doing so after work hours late into the night going onto the streets to befriend homeless folks around Singapore. Many times, he felt so tired and defeated. I remember once, I bumped into him on a MRT train. He started telling me how he has been hoping and praying so long for more Christians and, in particular, churches would step up in this area to serve the homeless in Singapore.

A few years later, in 2019, my team and I from Micah Singapore organised a conference (we call it Micah Conversation). We got my friend, the homeless ministry founder, to share. We also got another couple who had been opening their home to homeless youths.

Amidst all the participants were the pastors and leaders of a particular church. They were so struck, through the work of the Holy Spirit, by the faithfulness and love that these ministries showed to the homeless and troubled youth. After prayer and deliberation, the church leadership decided to operate a shelter to homeless people in the church premises. It has come to be known as S3Ps: Safe Sound Sleeping Places.

So, the church opened its homeless shelter around the end of 2019. This was probably only the first or second Protestant church which had opened its premises as a homeless shelter.

Then in early 2020, the Covid-19 pandemic struck. After that, a circuit breaker or lockdown was imposed in Singapore.

The church became filled up with homeless persons who had nowhere else to go. And there were too many for the one shelter to house them.

Many other churches stepped forward to open their premises also as homeless shelters.

The church shared their experience, knowledge, and processes with these many other churches—I think 20-30 churches—to go do likewise.

So, in the pandemic, there were suddenly many churches who housed the homeless. Even after the pandemic restrictions were lifted a few years later, there are still many churches continuing the work of serving the homeless.

The church's members would volunteer to go every night to befriend the homeless stayers, talk to them, hear their stories, attend to their concerns. Some of the church members cooked food for them and held special celebrations for the stayers.

The church has seen stayers come and go. Stayers who have moved on to find permanent housing, find jobs, and rebuild their lives. Also, stayers who return to the streets or get into trouble.

The church has also seen stayers who experienced the love of God. Some stayers have told the church volunteers they recognised that what the church and the volunteers are doing is from Jesus.

I share this story not as an example of how great things are. There have been many mistakes made along the way, I'm sure. And a cynic would say, how deep would the impact or transformation be? How many homeless can the churches help? How long term a solution is this? That's not the point of the ministries I mentioned, nor the point of this story.

However, I observe a few things.

DOES ANYTHING MATTER? WHY A CHRISTIAN SHOULD STILL CARE IN A WORLD OF DESPAIR

God-Orchestrated

First, so many things were not human planned. They were instead, **God-orchestrated**.

With human planning, there's only so much control we can exercise. So many resources we can avail ourselves of. But God can and will do far more and more creatively. God is eager to fulfil His plans and purposes. So, He wants us to be faithful to flow with His plans and His purposes. And the first and last task in this is to obey His word and pray.

We like to think of our God-given spiritual vocations in technical terms. Like building a physical structure. Or in formulas, as if they are computer code. If we do X, we will see Y. But God uses organic metaphors. Like growing and tending to a vine. I've tried growing plants many times. And I keep failing to keep them alive. It's not rocket science. But it takes a combination of many factors which are not within my control in order to succeed. It takes patience and attentive tending to. It takes careful compliance with instructions. But even so, it could fail. A pest might come along. Sickness might plague the plant. The weather could change. In this reality, one can only pray. So it is with spiritual work.

DOES ANYTHING MATTER? WHY A CHRISTIAN SHOULD STILL CARE IN A WORLD OF DESPAIR

What fruitfulness is

Second, was there fruitfulness?
I think so. There was a multiplication of Christians and ministries involved in serving the homeless.

Have they grown in spiritual maturity and character, that being a mark of spiritual fruit? I believe so. Because they have exhibited sacrificial love, which is the sign of obedience and spiritual maturity. Church members step forward to give of themselves, give of their attention and presence, sharing food, sharing stories, sharing life.

Fruitfulness is when we ourselves grow in spiritual maturity. When we grow in love for God and His. Grow in love, joy, peace, patience, kindness, gentleness, goodness, faithfulness, and self-control.

Also, there was a multiplication of homeless people who were served. This is another mark of spiritual fruit—the effect of good works on others. When more people experience the love of God through us. When more people experience the shalom–the wellbeing, goodness, peace–of the Kingdom of God manifested through our work. When more people experience a foretaste of God's coming Kingdom. Even if it is just a brief taste. Enough to get them on a quest for the Kingdom. This, I believe, is what Jesus meant by the "greater works" than His which we shall do (John 14:9-14). Works which reveal and glorify God.

Fruitfulness is when others experience the love and shalom of God through us. Fruitfulness is when people experience a foretaste of God's coming Kingdom.

Faithfulness of a few to the fruitfulness of many

How did it begin?
With the faithfulness of the individuals who faithfully ploughed in their homeless and care ministries. Even when they felt alone. Even when they could see no fruit. Even when they felt despair.

Faithfulness in praying and obeying God's word to love people sacrificially.

So, we see the **faithfulness of a few bringing about the fruitfulness of many. All orchestrated by God.**

In a recent church retreat, I was again contemplating this passage and struggling with God again about whether and to what extent I have borne fruit and done such "greater works". In the time of solitude and reflection our church members were directed to have, I felt God showing me an image of a trellis for a grapevine. I felt God telling me that such "greater works" take different forms for different Christians. For me, the work I do may be more systemic, upstream, whereas for others it may be more direct, and personal, e.g. sowing seeds and harvesting fruits. The latter may get to see the fruits of their hands more, because their kind of work is closer to the fruits. But the one who builds the trellis for the vineyard may not. Yet, it is work that is just as important.

It is easy for us to be discouraged if we do not get to frequently see the fruit borne from our works of service unto God. But we can pray and ask God to show us and encourage us that the work we are doing is in fact the "greater works" that He's prepared for us to participate in. If not, then to show us what we must do. If yes, then to rest in the knowledge that we are doing what He has given us to do, even if we do not see the fruit of our hands.

Faithful in the dark

I'm sure many of the individuals involved in these ministries would never have realised the bigger picture of how God orchestrated these different instruments and harmony lines together to produce this divine symphony. It so happened that I was a spectator of sorts at the different key points in this story. I'm sure there are many other parts unseen.

The point is that often, we will not get to see or know for sure the fruit that will be borne from our labour. This is the default perspective for all of us.

But God sees all. He is the God of eternity and an infinite possibilities. God is the fruit grower. He is the vine dresser. He is also the one working in us to give life, to bring transformational impact to others, to produce fruit that will last unto eternity.

He just wants us to be faithful to abide in Him, that we will flow with His purposes and plans. And He alone will take care of the fruitfulness. Even when no one sees anything. Even in the darkness.

We are called to **be faithful in the dark**.

Just like a baby growing in the darkness of the mother's womb. The mother does not see her child, nor how much her child has grown over the past day, or whether what she ate yesterday will go towards the child's growth. So it is with our ever-journeying self, and the work of our hands.

We may not realise how a gentle word spoken, or how the thing we did when no one was watching, could cause a series of ripples in the interwoven fabric of life, resulting in consequences that lasts unto eternity. In the unseen realm, quantum particles become eternally entangled and dance to the symphony of a divine masterpiece.

When the New Creation unrolls, and we arrive at the redeemed City, the New Heavens and New Earth, and we stand before God in worship, you may turn and notice someone you find vaguely familiar. And you will soon realise that that's the person your life, your work, your word has impacted. And not just that person, and not just your work. But also their family down the generations. But also the work of many others like yourself, who had doubted in the dark whether anything they did amidst all the uncertainty and difficulty had any impact at all.

I think of the song "Thank You" by Ray Boltz, which a pastor friend introduced. An excerpt of the lyrics goes:

> "I dreamed I went to heaven
> And you were there with me
> We walked upon the streets of gold
> Beside the crystal sea
> We heard the angels singing
> Then someone called your name
> You turned and saw this young man
> And he was smiling as he came
> And he said friend you may not know me now
> And then he said but wait
> You used to teach my Sunday School
> When I was only eight
> And every week you would say a prayer
> Before the class would start
> And one day when you said that prayer
> I asked Jesus in my heart
> Thank you for giving to the Lord".

And that, I think, is the assurance Jesus gave to us as His parting word.

That faithfulness in prayer and obedience to His Word expressed through sacrificial love will bring fruitfulness. He will guarantee it Himself. Because He wants the fruit, the abundant fruit for the harvest of life.

I'M REMINDED OF THE account of how one of the most well-regarded evangelists of the 19th century, Dwight L. Moody, became a Christian. After he stopped formal education in fifth grade, he worked in his uncle's retail shoe store as a salesman. His uncle made his employment conditional upon attendance at a church, to keep him from mischief. His Sunday School teacher Edward Kimball, being concerned about the darkness of his spiritual condition, visited Moody at the shoe store and shared with him the love of Christ. Shortly thereafter, Moody believed and followed Jesus. He went on to become a successful businessman, start various Sunday School and other ministries as well as Bible schools, and became a successful evangelist.[18]

The story goes that Moody's preaching and ministry led one Frederic B. Meyer to follow and preach Jesus. Meyer's preaching led J. Wilbur Chapman to pursue his calling to be an evangelist. One of the volunteers who helped Chapman in his evangelistic rallies was Billy Sunday, who learned to preach and evangelise from Chapman. Billy Sunday's preaching brought many to follow Jesus. A group of Christian businessmen were so inspired by Billy Sunday's evangelistic rallies that they invited an evangelist Mordecai Ham to hold a series in their city. A 16-year-old who attended was so stirred he gave his life to Jesus. That boy was Billy Graham. Billy Graham would eventually come to Singapore and hold a series of evangelistic rallies, which brought many to follow Jesus. Many of them would go on to become pastors and leaders of the Singapore Church.

I have not been able to verify every aspect of this account. However, we do know that Billy Graham himself had written about the profound impact of Moody's evangelistic ministry on him. Others have written about how Graham was the spiritual successor of Moody.

And it all started with a Sunday School teacher who was faithful in his ministry, obedient to God in preaching Jesus to his students, and doing so with great love.

Your joy will be full

And here's the promise of Jesus, if you remain faithful to this word: "11 These things I have spoken to you, that my joy may be in you, and that your joy may be full."

Joy is not pleasure. Joy is not pride. Joy is not happiness. Joy is not achievement. Joy is not success.

Joy is satisfaction from being exactly what you're supposed to be, doing exactly what you are supposed to do, from knowing that you are right there in the centre of God's will. Joy is to experience the satisfaction of God. Joy is to be in the Lord always (Philippians 4:4).

WE RETURN, THEN, TO the beginning. For joy comes when the Word spoken to you germinates in your spirit. This is, after all, the Word that made the world. That made you. That is remaking you. You who are 'not yet' but, with the seed of eternity planted within, embracing the eternal Word that lights your world. Even if it is only light that comes through the size of a pinhole. It is light enough to see the coming world which is waiting to meet your present. So, press on to live, to believe, to work, to keep, to tend to what God has made. To choose compassion. To be a neighbour. To care. To pray. To obey. To love sacrificially. Faithfully.

For faithfulness brings fruitfulness.

Be faithful even in the dark. There is light enough.

May your joy ever be full in Christ.

Prayer For Those Who Choose to Continue the Struggle with Doubt, Despair or Futility

O Heavenly Father, Lord Jesus, Holy Spirit,
    I am weak and weary.
I bear doubt and despair.
Let your light in for me to see
Enough for me to care.
Help me keep your Word
And tend to those you've made;
Choose the way of love
In faith, for hope's sake.
Let me gaze through the abyss
On the first fruits of Resurrection.
Let my dry bones live.
Remake me into your New Creation.
Amen.

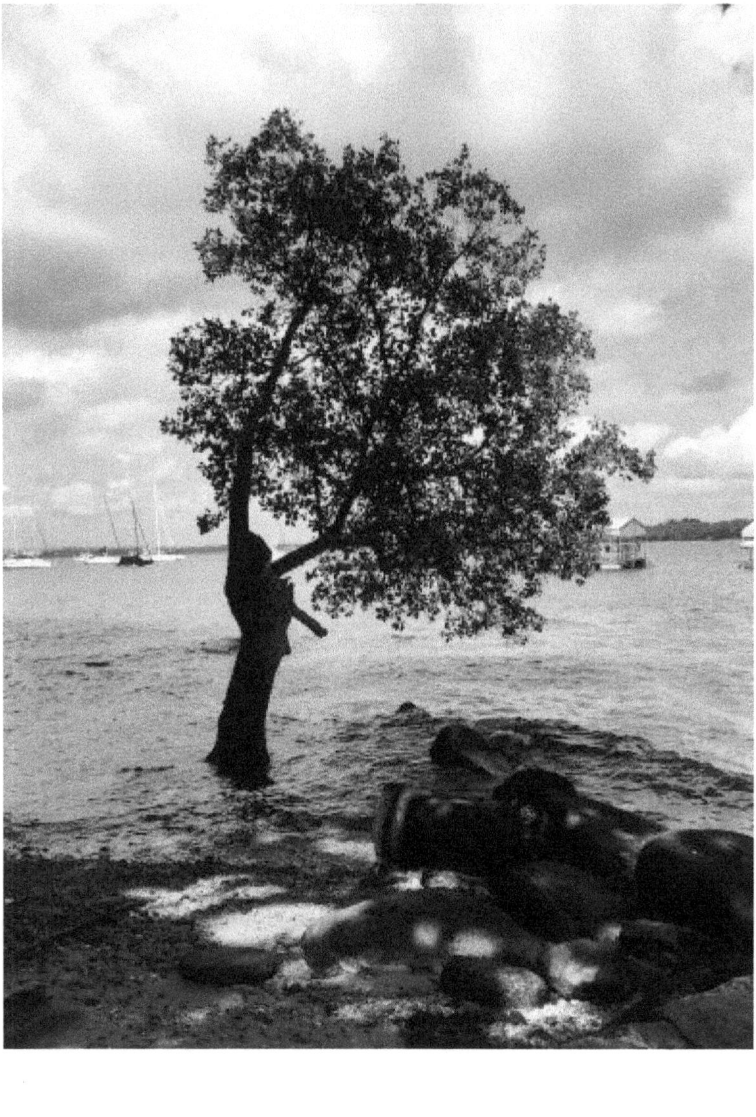

Support

If you'd like to support a charity which, among other things, serves and journeys with homeless persons, do consider supporting Bless Community Services, which I presently serve as Chairperson of.

More information can be found here:

www.bless.org.sg/donation[1]

If you do make a donation, please state in the remarks for tracking purposes: "RWBOOKDAM".

Thank you for your support in our work.

---

1. http://www.bless.org.sg/donation

[1] All names of individuals in this book have been changed.

[2] https://education.nationalgeographic.org/resource/isaac-newton-who-he-was-why-apples-are-falling/#[2]

[3] Hard or causal determinism could pose a moral problem for human society. Because if someone came up to me today, punched me senselessly and robbed me of all my money, what could we as a society say? We would have to concede that his acts were the result of past physical events tracing back to the beginning of the universe. It is not his own moral choice. It is not actually his intention. And so, he should not be held accountable for his actions.

Can we even justify having a justice system at all? Proponents of hard determinism would say, although the robber should not be *blamed*, he should go to jail nonetheless to keep everyone else safe and to reform him. But why would that be necessary or worthy? Since the supposed wrongdoing was never his intention anyway but the product of physical causes beyond him, there is nothing about him that should be changed. And there is no way to say that he wouldn't do the same thing again if he went to jail for a while.

I am aware that there is a range of various views on how people can be held morally responsible even if there is hard determinism. Some 'compatibilist' views suggest that moral responsibility exists as long as a person is not subject to external constraints in choosing one's actions. Other views hold that people can be held morally responsible even if they could not have chosen otherwise; so long as they voluntarily made the choice. Others focus on the reactive emotions or attitudes towards people's behaviour. And others consider that as a matter of necessity and social policy, we would have to hold people accountable even if there is no basis for metaphysical moral foundations. I will not venture to address any of these since the issue of moral responsibility is not the point of raising the issue of determinism. The point is what follows: that it may seem like there's no point taking action at all.

[4] Here lies a leap from hard determinism to fatalism, which does not necessarily follow and should not be equated.

[5] https://papers.ssrn.com/sol3/papers.cfm?abstract_id=3918955

[6] https://sg.style.yahoo.com/why-do-young-singaporeans-not-want-to-have-children-052951884.html; https://www.channelnewsasia.com/singapore/birth-rate-fertility-rate-children-kids-marriage-parenthood-3354451

---

2. https://education.nationalgeographic.org/resource/isaac-newton-who-he-was-why-apples-are-falling/

[7] https://aeon.co/ideas/humans-are-the-only-animals-who-crave-oblivion-through-suicide

[8] https://psycnet.apa.org/record/1974-32695-001; https://journals.plos.org/plosone/article?id=10.1371/journal.pone.0249896

[9] Frederick Buechner, "Secrets in the Dark: A Life in Sermons" (March 13, 2007, HarperCollins).

[10] https://cct.biola.edu/implausibility-of-physical-determinism/; https://thereader.mitpress.mit.edu/determinism-classical-argument-against-free-will-failure/

[11] Since these realisations, critics of free will began to change their argument and assert that physical indeterminacy and randomness disprove free will, because it would mean all our choices are subject to some random forces and are thus meaningless. But probabilities do not necessarily equate to randomness.

In any case, I think focusing on the apparent tension between determinism and free will is unhelpful. Instead, the more important question is whether human beings have agency, whether or not people do have or experience free will (whatever that means) or whether determinism—whether hard or soft determinism—is true. Is it possible then that human beings have agency, and human consciousness, irrespective? After all, even secular philosophers like Thomas Nagel (Mind & Cosmos) argue that human consciousness remains to be explained and cannot be accounted for on a purely materialistic view of the universe. If the mind is not nothing but the brain, and consciousness is more than merely physical forces at work, then there is yet more to it than whatever limitations which hard determinism may demand we believe. As a Christian, I would certainly not be able to accept that the universe is nothing but physical things and forces.

[12] https://www.straitstimes.com/singapore/holding-the-hand-of-a-dying-stranger

[13] Frederick Buechner, Alphabet of Grace, (March 10, 2009, HarperOne).

[14] https://www.mdpi.com/2077-1444/11/4/192; https://aeon.co/essays/what-can-augustine-of-hippos-philosophy-teach-us-about-hope

[15] https://www.christianitytoday.com/better-samaritan/2023/february/coral-reefs-creation-care-and-hope-of-resurrection.html

[16] https://files.eric.ed.gov/fulltext/EJ1149537.pdf

[17] https://www.ft.com/content/ffb1edb2-9db5-11e5-b45d-4812f209f861; https://theworld.org/stories/2015-10-06/refugee-girl-who-changed-merkels-mind-where-she-now

[18] https://www.moody.edu/about/our-bold-legacy/d-l-moody/

About the Author

Ronald JJ Wong is a practising lawyer and Deputy Managing Director of his law firm, the National Coordinator of a Christian mission mobilisation movement, Board member of a mission humanitarian organisation, caretaker of a Christian arts and culture community, an Elder of his local church, and Chairman of a social service agency. He is the author of The Justice Demand: Social Justice & The Singapore Church, co-editor of Good News for Bruised Reeds, Vol. 1: Walking with Same-Sex Attracted Friends, Vol. 2: Mental Health & The Gospel Community, and Vol. 3: Colours of the Kingdom, and co-editor of Assault on the Body: Sexual Violence and the Gospel Community.

Read more at https://www.ronaldjjwong.com.

Milton Keynes UK
Ingram Content Group UK Ltd.
UKHW051851300624
444825UK00004B/153